The series editors:

Ronald Carter is Professor of Modern English Language in the Department of English Studies at the University of Nottingham and is the editor of the Routledge INTERFACE series in Language and Literary Studies. He is also co-author of *The Routledge History of Literature in English*. From 1989 to 1992 he was seconded as National Director for the Language in the National Curriculum (LINC) project, directing a £21.4 million in-service teacher education programme.

Angela Goddard is Senior Lecturer in Language at the Centre for Human Communication, Manchester Metropolitan University, and was Chief Moderator for the project element of English Language A-level for the Northern Examination and Assessment Board (NEAB) from 1983 to 1995. Her publications include *The Language Awareness Project: Language and Gender*, vols I and II, 1988, and *Researching Language*, 1993 (Framework Press).

Core textbook:

Working with Texts: A core book for language analysis
Ronald Carter, Angela Goddard, Danuta Reah,
Keith Sanger, Maggie Bowring

Satellite titles:

The Language of Sport
Adrian Beard

The Language of Politics
Adrian Beard

The Language of Advertising: Written texts
Angela Goddard

Language and Gender
Angela Goddard and Lindsey Meân Patterson

The Language of Magazines
Linda McLoughlin

The Language of Poetry
John McRae

The Language of Newspapers
Danuta Reah

The Language of Humour
Alison Ross

The Language of Fiction
Keith Sanger

The Language of Drama
Keith Sanger

Related titles:

INTERFACE series:

Variety in Written English
Tony Bex

Language, Literature and Critical Practice
David Birch

A Linguistic History of English Poetry
Richard Bradford

The Language of Jokes
Delia Chiaro

The Discourse of Advertising
Guy Cook

Literary Studies in Action
Alan Durant and Nigel Fabb

English in Speech and Writing
Rebecca Hughes

Feminist Stylistics
Sara Mills

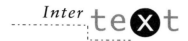

The Language of ICT

Information and communication technology

- Tim Shortis

LONDON AND NEW YORK

First published 2001
by Routledge
11 New Fetter Lane, London EC4P 4EE

Simultaneously published in the USA
and Canada
by Routledge
29 West 35th Street, New York, NY 10001

*Routledge is an imprint of the Taylor & Francis
Group*

© 2001 Tim Shortis

The right of Tim Shortis to be identified
as the Author of this Work has been
asserted by him in accordance with the
Copyright, Designs and Patents Act 1988

Typeset in Stone Sans/Stone Serif by
Solidus (Bristol) Limited

Printed and bound in Great Britain by
TJ International Ltd, Padstow, Cornwall

*British Library Cataloguing in Publication
Data*
A catalogue record for this book is
available from the British Library

*Library of Congress Cataloging in Publication
Data*

Shortis, Tim, 1958–
   The language of ICT/Tim Shortis.
      p. cm. – (Intertext)
   Includes bibliographical references
(p.) and index.
   1. Communication—Technological
innovations.   2. Discourse analysis.
3. Sublanguage.   4. Words, New.
5. Electronic data processing.
I. Title.   II. Intertext (London, England)
P96.T42 S448 2000   00-029104
302.2–dc21

ISBN 0–415–22275–3

contents

acknowledgements

Thanks to Angela Goddard for her encouragement and help throughout the writing of this book, to the Warden and Fellows of Merton College, Oxford, who gave me a studentship term to research and write, and to the Bodleian Library staff. Thank you also to my colleagues at Saint Brendan's, and to the students for their stimulating language investigation field-work. Finally, thanks to Jon Stevenson for his insights into chat.

This book is dedicated to George Keith and Ted Nelson, both visionary teachers in their different ways, and also to Maria, Sam, Pat, Michaelangelo and Kate.

The author and publishers thank the following for their permission to reprint copyright material: John Benjamins Publishing Company for extracts from Chris Werry, 'Linguistic and interactional features of Internet relay chat' in *Computer-Mediated Communication: Linguistic, social and cross cultural perspectives*, edited by Susan C. Herring (1996); Cambridge University Press for permission to adapt John Algeo's data on language change from the *Cambridge History of English Language* (1999); Helen Petrie for permission to adapt her tables from *Writing in Cyberspace*; Danuta Reah for the Colchester Chat Room; Kevin Eagles and Penny Price for permission to use a private email; Dell Computers for permission to use their 1997 marketing materials; Routledge for extracts from *Redesigning English*; Tempus Books and Ted Nelson for extracts from *Computer Lib*; Rough Guides and Angus Kennedy for the extract from *The Rough Guide to the Internet* (2000); Oxford University Press for the definition of 'spam' reprinted from *The Oxford Dictionary of New Words* (2nd edition, 1997); Melanie McGrath and Flamingo Books for the extracts from *Hard, Soft and Wet*; News International, *The Times* and the *Sunday Times*, London, for 'The day my computer died' by Magnus Linklater (1996) and for 'Internet Jargon Buster' (1996) and for 'Getting the message' by Peter Stanford (1999).

Every effort has been made to trace and seek permission from copyright holders. The publisher will be glad to hear from any such unacknowledged copyright holders.

A note on spelling

Throughout this book the spelling, capitalisation and hyphenation of words such as e-mail and Internet reflects the common UK standard forms of January 2000. These may well change, given the tendency of new words to drop such markers over time. (See Unit 7.)

abbreviations

ASCII code	American Standard Committee for Information Interchange
BNC	British National Corpus
BTW	by the way
CBT	computer-based training
CMC	computer-mediated communication
DTP	desktop publishing
f2f	face to face
GUI	graphical user interface
HTML	hypertext mark-up language
HTTP	hypertext transfer protocol
ICT	information and communication technology
IMHO	in my humble opinion
IRC	Internet relay chat
IRL	in real life (play on URL)
IT	information technology
IWD	interactive written discourse
KWIC list	key word in context list
MOO	MUD, object oriented
MUD	multi-user dungeon/domain (role-playing game)
NLP	natural language processing
ROTFL	rolling on the floor laughing
ROTFLOL	rolling on the floor laughing out loud
SGML	standard general mark-up language
TWAIN	thing with an interesting name
URL	uniform resource locator

introduction

Hype and evidence in the information revolution

It's more than hype: new technology is all around us, and there is no going back. Internet, e-mail, voice mail, chat rooms, CD-ROM drives, fax machines: we are surrounded by words, which are well understood and used by some people even though the words, objects and practices involved in their use did not exist even twenty years ago, and some may seem out of date in another ten years.

This book explores the social and linguistic features of the new types of text that have been made possible by computers. This includes considering the nature of the electronic word, the new varieties of text it is found in, and the apparent changes in human identity and communication. As with the other books in this series, this means having ways of describing patterns and features of language with relative precision, and then being able to interpret this information by relating it to its social perspectives.

As the media and advertisers constantly remind us, we are living in a time of rapid technological change that has been likened in impact to the industrial revolution of the nineteenth century. However, as with the industrial revolution, access to new technologies is very uneven. Even allowing for the extraordinary increase in e-mail use over the past five years, only 2 per cent of the world's population had these facilities in 1996, and even in the UK and the USA, countries with relatively high computer ownership, far fewer people have access to computers than have use of televisions, video recorders and telephones. While the gap may close, new technologies are still 'gated' by lines of affluence, power, education, age, and gender.[1,2] There is no homogeneous speech community where everyone's understanding is the same: individual experience of new communication technology texts, like anything else, varies widely and changes rapidly.[3]

However, technology is increasingly embedded in writing and publication processes. In the course of this book being made, people have sent faxes, left answerphone messages, 'scanned' documents, 'surfed the net', used 'search engines', used 'DTP programs' to set the text 'online', and replied to e-mail. In their leisure time they may have used 'cheats' on 'platform games' to get on to the next 'level'. Many of these new words are not 'in the dictionary' in the sense they are used here, but they are well understood by their 'users'. In all this we can see a language associated with new technologies emerging. This isn't just a set of words for newly invented consumer goods, like a new label for a better kind of toaster; we are learning to write, read, speak and listen in new ways as different kinds of communication are made possible by technological development.

Change is embedded in the way we see our identities as individuals, communities and communicators. We are creating so-called virtual identities and virtual audiences as the traditional constraints of time, geographical space, physical presence and national boundaries are altered by a **cyborg** fusion that is part technology, part human.[4] It all creates its own constraints too as technology insistently makes digital records of all this communication in vast data reserves, built up to be examined, or '**mined**', by those who have ownership and control over them. Supermarket loyalty cards trade discounts for access to such information about the spending habits of the loyal.[5]

New communication technologies are also the subject of a marketing and money-oriented discourse, which sells us promises about our future. Technology is driving rapid redistributions in property and power and creating extreme wealth for the businesses selling it. The virtual monopolies and oligopolies in some types of product supply, such as software, distort the way in which the technology is presented: the aim of the communication is shaped by its function to sell the goods. These commercial enterprises provide a vast data vault of texts and discourse, which can be studied and read against the grain of the original writers' intentions. Every software help tutorial which addresses its readers with examples and templates as if they were an American business employee is also providing a text for study about the way people are being represented and the underlying ideology associated with that.

The situation is unstable: communication technologies continue to change rapidly, both technically and in their associated communication practices. New technical possibilities lead to new types of text as people find different ways of communicating with each other, and through that to new social possibilities. This is shown most dramatically in the Internet: created by the US defence industry for the exchange of computer protocols written in code and only later used to carry the world wide web and new emerging genres of e-mails and websites written in human languages for non-military purposes. Conventions and genres continue to mutate in the light of practice and use.

New technology soon becomes old technology; one wave of innovation is succeeded by the next. So new words not in the dictionary now may have been replaced by the time the print dictionaries can categorise them. E-mail and Internet relay chat (IRC) may in time give way to video conferencing and keyboarded word processing may soon be superseded by the dictation modes of speech recognition. It can be hard to analyse the nature of new types of communication amidst all these tramplings of change. However, the very different kinds of technology have some underlying similarities in the way they change the material nature of information. In particular, they all 'technologise the word' to make information machine-readable: although the way it is read by the computer is different from the way we read it. As the word is technologised, information becomes **commodified**: turned into a fluidly transferable, linkable commodity that can be seamlessly pasted into other texts that have no connection with the original purposes and contexts and that can then be searched electronically.

Academic focus on the language of new communication and information technology is relatively recent but there is a small, rapidly growing body of research as academics start to describe and classify IT texts from linguistic, sociological and cross-cultural points of view: some of the better known books, articles and electronic sources are listed in the Bibliography and are updated on our website: netting-it.com However, the research coverage is still sketchy and uneven. The comments Susan Herring made over five years ago about computer-mediated communication still apply: 'futuristic speculation and popular stereotyping still far outstrip the availability of factual information' and there is 'a pressing need for descriptive and empirical research', which this book seeks to promote.[6]

Information and communication technology texts show language changing in a microcosm and computers can be used to track these changes in some detail. This book seeks to encourage investigations beyond the claims of pundits and to make a small contribution to the descriptive and empirical work referred to by Herring. Such research has its problems and opens opportunities: it can be exciting to investigate aspects of language use for which there is no agreed body of knowledge or method. This book provides frameworks for thinking about the topic, and a few lenses and filters to help a methodical focus on the language features of technology texts: features which can be obscured by the wordy claims of marketing and packaging presentation. IT is technically complex but it doesn't take the techno-wizardry of a systems analyst to reflect on its social and linguistic dimensions.

There is a selection of example texts and active links for each chapter on the website: netting-it.com

What is IT? – the nature of electronic text

Aims of this unit

What are ICT texts, what do they have in common and how can they be categorised? This unit identifies some different types of new technology text and the different properties they share because of the electronic or digital words that make them up. By its material nature electronic text allows new ways of reading and writing information including electronic searches, links and records.

Old technologies were once new

Types of text change as technology changes, and they always have done: even handwriting depends on the technologies of writing materials from slate to quill and pen, and the invention of printing in the fifteenth century developed the importance of the written word as never before. It is easy to forget that a book is a kind of technology; it is just that the ways of using it are now taken for granted by most literate adults. The computer theorist Ted Nelson makes the point humorously in this aside about computer jargon.

This book is a multi-user, high resolution, demand-paged, hardware–software, read mostly memory, retrieval and display system with realtime interaction, tactile interface, audio and video feedback.

    See?

    Don't be afraid of technical terms.[1]

People refer to a 'new kind of language' in e-mail or on the Internet and there is a popular view that new technology is changing communication. If such ideas are more than loose talk then they raise questions about what is meant by 'language' in this context. Certainly, technology has created lots of technical terms but then so have cars, carburettors and gas turbine engines; a lexicon of specialist terminology may not amount to a new language. Computer language is sometimes said to be different in terms of appearance and form. Are such keyboard shortcuts as 'CyaL8r' in a different language from 'See you later' or are they just different ways of writing a known language? Are **smileys** and **emoticons** verbal language, new punctuation or visual gestures, and how fixed is the boundary between language and communication anyway?

    One aspect of new communication technology that does seem to be different is the way information is stored: the material nature of electronic records.

Activity

The following is a list of some types of new technical consumer products that have emerged over the last fifteen years. Which would you categorise as new communication technologies? For example, which have allowed new kinds of text and interaction and what kinds of text and interaction have they allowed? Which **digitise** information and make it machine-readable and transferable and which use electronic forms of human language such as letters and numbers?

1 MP3 recorder;	8 audio CD-player;
2 Mini-disk;	9 cyberpet;
3 satellite dish;	10 digital camera;
4 fax machine;	11 washing machine with microchip
5 digital TV;	computer-operated controls;
6 multi-media computer;	12 mobile phone.
7 platform game console;	

Commentary

Looking at these examples we can see a distinction between tech-nologies that allow machine-to-machine communication, those that allow machine-to-human communication, and those that enable computer-mediated human-to-human communication (CMC).

Several items seem like improved versions of previous technologies but there are differences in the way they store information in a common format: in some cases this is digital but not necessarily verbal (an MP3 audio file), in others the information is in human language but is not machine-readable (a handwritten fax) and in others the information is stored electronically and is readable by humans and by computers. The camera isn't new, but the way it stores information is, and gives it a common informational language with the multi-media computer. The mobile telephone appears similar to its wired predecessors except that it moves private communication into public space. Its electronic address books involve creating computer text records. The computer word processor digitises information in machine codes and displays human language.

What do ICT texts have in common?

New communication technologies are characterised by electronic storage and transfer of information to other machines in compatible forms although the way such information is read by humans and machines is always distinctly different even where the computer's programmed impersonation of sense suggests otherwise. The power and limitations of ICT text lie in this strange cyborg interface of the machine-readable and human-readable, as we shall see.

ICT texts tend to have a dual audience of computer programming coded language for machines and verbal language for reading by human beings. Sometimes these come together when the human language matches a computer command as in the instruction 'Delete'; but this is no more than a machine simulation of human communication. The signal that tells the telephone answering machine to respond to a call is not the same as the auditory signal that tells you the telephone is ringing. In many personal computers machine language and human language meet in the ASCII extended character set code. This is used to write lines of computer instructions and to write human type. You can see either side by side if you look at the reveal codes option in a word processor, or at a web page in text form or if you open a text with the wrong set of filters. These computer instructions are what programmers call high level languages but ultimately they relate to the binary on-off language of machine code. So each letter will have a pattern of binary code associated with it, as in the table below.

Table 1.1 ASCII codes for the English alphabet (omitting control codes)

Code No	Letter	Code No	Letter	Code No	Letter	Code No	Letter	Code No	Letter
32	(spc)	51	3	70	F	89	Y	108	l
33	!	52	4	71	G	90	Z	109	m
34	"	53	5	72	H	91	[	110	n
35	#	54	6	73	I	92	\	111	o
36	$	55	7	74	J	93	]	112	p
37	%	56	8	75	K	94	^	113	q
38	&	57	9	76	L	95	–	114	r
39	'	58	:	77	M	96	`	115	s
40	(	59	;	78	N	97	a	116	t
41	)	60	<	79	O	98	b	117	u
42	*	61	=	80	P	99	c	118	v
43	+	62	>	81	Q	100	d	119	w
44	,	63	?	82	R	101	e	120	x
45	-	64	@	83	S	102	f	121	y
46	.	65	A	84	T	103	g	122	z
47	/	66	B	85	U	104	h	123	{
48	0	67	C	86	V	105	I	124		
49	1	68	D	87	W	106	j	125	}
50	2	69	E	88	X	107	k	126	~

Unlike the science fiction character Hal in *2001: A Space Odyssey*, computers and human beings read text in a very different manner, even if this is disguised by the semblance of interaction which may be taking place on the screen messages. When my word processor 'asks' me if I am writing a letter, if I am 'sure' I 'want to save Betty.doc' or suggests I've used a sentence that is too long, it simulates the kind of comment which might be made by a person, but the basis of its intervention is entirely mechanistic. To put it brutally, the computer pattern matches **text strings** of code and then carries out a number of programmed instructions in response to that pattern match.

The implications of machine-readable cyborg text

Such electronic storage of words creates opportunities to copy and re-use information seamlessly: a word-processed message can be edited and re-used as part of the screen messages which appear when the computer is turned on; private e-mail can be edited and expanded as part of a page of a website with a mass audience and the same can happen to a video, as in the notorious Pamela Anderson websites. An answerphone message can be recorded as a voice clip and inserted into a multi-media document. All electronic texts can be endlessly linked to each other and to other types of information and computation processes.

Properties of electronic text

The machine-readable nature of new technology text enables information to be manipulated, giving ICT texts a number of properties that make them materially different from recordings of sound, or writing on paper. These properties include the following: plasticity, links, tagging, searches, templates, footprint records and virtual identities.

Plasticity: ICT, and especially word processing, generates screen text, or softcopy, which is impermanent and available to be altered, remodelled or combined. In the past the written record has been seen as something having fixity. Many ICT texts are only as fixed as their last screen image or printout.

Links: Text can be copied and combined with every other type of compatible ICT text and image. This allows the creation of very large, infinitely malleable, informationally linked systems of information. Such texts can be **multi-modal** with animated combinations of visual, auditory, graphical and verbal information. This is at the heart of multi-media.

Tagging: IT texts can be tagged so that particular sequences of information are associated with other types of information. For example, a text can be framed by commands so that it has a particular status and appearance on the screen, or a word in a computer language corpus can be tagged with its part of speech. Such organisation underpins the structures of hypertext documents such as web pages and allows complex searches of linked information.

Searches: Following on from this, computers can be programmed to match up patterns of code, allowing complex searches of vast archives of text material to be undertaken very quickly. This is what allows the

9

ludicrously swift reference to information in CD-ROMs or web browsers. The reference work for the *Oxford English Dictionary* or for concordances such as those of Shakespeare or the Bible,[2] which took decades of scholars' work can now be completed much more quickly.[3] The particular string may also trigger a sequence of processes or commands. Thus, a particular text string may trigger a set of computer-animated responses. So in a spellchecker, a text string not recognised will trigger a dialogue box of options. Like an electronic version of a Heath Robinson cartoon, the board game Mousetrap, or a marble run – a text string can trigger a sequence of electronic consequences. For example, the inclusion of the word 'arse' in a GCSE social science website will automatically render it inaccessible in a school intranet,[4] and coming from Scunthorpe barred one e-mailer from being able to use his America Online account![5]

Templates: Many IT texts simulate human interaction by using a template which approximates the norms of a particular type of human-to-human communication. Thus bank teller machines will create an electronic loop or flow diagram that models particular types of service encounter and a word processor 'wizard' may prompt a writer for addresses and other types of information which are expected in formal letters. Electronic text makes its own record of the structure (template/ frame) and material (text), both of which can be re-worked seamlessly in ways beyond their original function.

Footprints: Many IT texts make electronic 'footprint' records of various types which can be traced and used later.[6] At the most basic level, electronic text can be saved and copied. But new technologies may also keep records other than the main text. Even a fax will send a 'footprint' record of when it was sent and from where. Loyalty cards provided by stores allow retailers to build up a very detailed database of the purchasing habits of their users. Similarly, Internet service providers can log the accumulating patterns of use of their customers and sell the information to advertisers and market researchers. Even word processors commonly record how long has been spent on a document and the call centre equivalent can enable managers to monitor the call duration and 'efficiency' of staff.

Virtuality: IT texts can create a parallel world that simulates the real (IRL) without being anchored in the constraints of a physical context. They can have live real-time links with disparate and geographically remote audiences, information and media. A word-processed document can be updated automatically with information from a remote source without human agency. People may communicate intimately without disclosing cues about their identity such as their sex, voice or appearance. A **bot** such as Eliza may simulate human communication successfully and without detection.

Power and technological literacy

IT texts create new dynamics of power where access to knowledge about how the system works can confer status and practical powers to determine the access and membership of others. This is at its clearest in the **hacker** subculture or the Wizards and Opers (systems operator) refereeing multi-user dungeons (MUD) or Internet relay chat (IRC). At a more mundane level, the users' familiarity with how to use IRC emoticons and their typing speed may determine access to Internet chat.

Written text, particularly in its printed form, has been associated with power, authority and permanent records – but this is changing. In one of the earlier studies of new technology texts, Michael Herne observed the way in which new technology works to 'undermine and deconstruct the literate text'.[7] Herne noted that a text on screen lacks the property of fixity and can become completely malleable: alive, linkable and permanently subject to change in the 'soft copy' electronic form. 'An act of reading can so easily become an act of re-writing.' He also observed that technological development would give more people direct access to the print production processes needed to produce hard copy (published documents). This would take away some of the status currently associated with printed text.[8]

Typically IT texts lower the threshold of access to publishing of all kinds. Cheaper sophisticated technology dissolves some of the traditional obstructions to publication and expands the potential repertoire of users. Thus far more people are now able to 'publish documents' with high production values or co-ordinate complex information on the Internet with a potentially vast audience. IT texts give writers control of texts which combine diverse media, allowing for the creation of new genres of communication which blur traditional partitions. One of the complaints made about the Internet is that it is an open text-publishing forum with few controls on access.[9]

Participative reading and constraints

New forms of information texts, because of their vertical or hierarchical organisation of material, encourage new styles of reading where the reader makes their own journey across the text and its related links. Conventional paper-based text often invited a directed sequence of starting at the beginning, turning the page and following the author's intentions in order to the end. Alternatively, there was a type of reference reading of looking up a particular entry. Reading the end of a thriller or disclosing its ending might be seen as cheating or spoiling by that model. A reader 'journeying' in hypertext reads like a writer, negotiating their pathways of sequence and chosen links. And by saving the sequence of links they make through a text they can recreate the text in their own exploration of it.

IT texts also place a number of constraints on their creators forcing them into cyborg (human–machine interface) relationships with their electronic tools in which they have to meet the protocols of the machine for the information to be accepted by it. Information needs to be 'inputted' in a way the computer recognises, both in the form of the response and the sequencing on the loop. So for example, an answer-phone message will not 'hear' you until the record space in its sequence and the hole in the wall machine will similarly constrain the kind of communication it wishes to entertain to a 'menu' of options. Perhaps the single most important constraint is the keyboard: most information is inputted with a keyboard and, where it is not, as in the case of speech recognition technology for word processors, the sound signal is pattern matched with its likely ASCII written equivalent. This is what leads to the peculiar response of speech recognition technology which may record dictated text accurately for much of the time and then translate a laugh as 'Eiffel Tower'.[10] Similarly, at the time of writing, true handwriting recognition has given way to types of handwriting which ensure that the user's letter formation will be recognised by the machine. Many of the innovations in new language styles come from keyboard constraints.

Activity

Collect some examples of the following types of new text and discourse which would not have existed thirty years ago. Consider these in the light of the properties described. To what extent do they show the features mentioned? In particular look out for those aspects of the text that contained digitised information and those aspects which contain machine readable ASCII-related text.

1 word-processed letter;
2 e-mail;
3 website;
4 handwritten fax;
5 word-processed fax;
6 recording of a mobile
   telephone call;
7 Internet chat;
8 answerphone message (tape or
   digital);
9 electronic 'talking' toy (e.g.
   Amazing Amy or Furby);
10 CD-ROM encyclopaedia;
11 helpline on a computer program.

Commentary

You may notice such differences as the way in which the handwritten fax contains electronic storage of information that is not machine-readable whereas the word-processed fax is all machine-readable. The multi-media encyclopedia may contain information of both types.

Summary

From this unit you will have identified certain repeating features of the new text types made possible by recent technological innovation: you might be developing your prototype model of a new technology text which has some of the following features:

1   Electronic storage and transmission of diverse information.
2   Includes electronic typed text and/or digitised information.
3   Allows instant communication across geographical space.
4   Can be linked to other electronic texts and processes.
5   Keeps a record of its 'history' automatically.
6   Echoes previous genres and technologies.

ICT allows new ways of composition in which information can be copied and re-used seamlessly for new purposes and audiences. You may be starting to think about the way new technology texts undermine the traditional notions of fixity, permanent record and authority associated with the written word in the age of print.

Extension

1   Electronic service encounters. Investigate one of the new technology text types such as a hole in the wall bank machine interaction or voice mail. Note or transcribe some of the sequences to make a record of their messages and see if you can reconstruct a flow diagram of their loop of discourse. How similar are these to their equivalent f2f (face-to-face) human interactions? What are the language devices these machines use to simulate human interaction? Look out for terms of address and politeness markers.[11]

Laying IT out – graphology and multi-modal texts

Aims of this unit

In the first unit we looked at the way in which developments in information technology make it easier for people to produce multi-modal texts combining words and images. This unit looks at what we can learn from the appearance or graphology of new technology including its impact on desktop published documents and the emergence of new patterns of punctuation, spelling, and use of symbols in computer-mediated communication (CMC). New technology texts seem to reflect changes in the nature and status of the visual markings of text. Graphology may also function unwittingly to record aspects of the semi-automated communication process. Finally, we look at aspects of the visual and kinaesthetic in Internet texts.

Text analysis and the clues given by layout

Traditional approaches to textual study have tended to emphasise the importance of verbal features of language in written texts over features of layout and presentation. From that perspective, graphology, literally, the marks on the page, has been less valued for itself than for what it reveals about other formal aspects of a text: its words (lexis), grammar (syntax and morphology), meanings (semantics) and overall structure (discourse).

Graphology is important in signalling **tenor** (or the implied social relationship between the text and the reader). Even in a word-processed letter, a font can act like clothing to indicate attitudes of formality, friendliness, tradition and innovation. Graphology can also indicate structure by signalling how information is arranged, chunked and sequenced (discourse).[1]

More recently, some linguists have argued that the visual has been ignored because language has been treated as a discrete abstract entity.[2] In practice language is embedded in communication, and some of that overall communication will be non-verbal. Everyday awareness will tell us that advertisers, for example, devote great energy to graphology, and paralinguistic features, and the verbal supports the image rather than the other way around; or as Kress puts it, writing is 'pushed into the margin'. Furthermore, social changes, along with the technical facilities created by communication technology, have started to change the nature of texts and literacies by enabling types of text which combine words and image in new dynamics. The graphological can be electronically hooked to the structural aspects, as in hypertext and outlining, leading to new ways of reading and responding to text as in the grading of websites for qualities such as 'interactivity' and 'navigation'. According to Goodman,[3] the strong tradition of 'prioritising the strictly verbal over the pictorial' has given way to a tradition in which texts combine 'devices from more than one semiotic mode of communication simultaneously'. Because IT texts lower the thresholds of access to complex production techniques the look of the page is 'not a matter only for a specialised group of designers of texts' but a 'general concern and the means for the page design are already there'.[4]

New technology texts are most obviously new in their appearance. One fundamental difference is that text is composed on a screen instead of paper. It may be positioned next to a graphic or linked electronically to other information. It may be published on paper, as an e-mail enclosure or combined with other types of imagery. It can be animated so it moves. Links to other programs, choices of font, use of white space, and space shifting give a vast choice of graphic and multi-modal possibilities by comparison with a typed document or handwriting and they make it harder to separate out verbal language from communication.

Activity

Study the following notice which was composed by an IT technician in a college. What do you notice about the language, the layout, and the relationship between the two?

15

Text: Virus Alert

VIRUS ALERT

YOUR WORK IS AT RISK!

IF WHEN YOU TRY TO USE YOUR FLOPPY DISK AN ALARM GOES OFF

.... STOP ....

- **TAKE YOUR DISK OUT OF THE FLOPPY DRIVE IMMEDIATELY AND FIND AN I.T. TECHNICIAN**
- **Do NOT USE THE DISK AGAIN UNTIL IT HAS BEEN CHECKED BY AN I.T. TECHNICIAN**

YOUR SAVED WORK ON THE FLOPPY DISK IS AT RISK FROM BEING IRRECOVERABLY DAMAGED IF YOU DO NOT FOLLOW THESE INSTRUCTIONS.

DO NOT SWITCH ON ANY COMPUTER WITH A FLOPPY DISK IN THE DRIVE

DO NOT RESET OR REBOOT ANY COMPUTER WITH A FLOPPY DISK IN THE DRIVE

16

Commentary

This desktop published notice was written and produced by an IT technician in a college in the mid-1990s. It was used as a poster on the walls in the rooms which had computers, before being reduced in size as a notice to be attached to all disks sold in the college. It has also been adapted and used as a screensaver. It is typical of the kind of desktop published notices seen in all sorts of institutions and work places.

It would have been difficult to make this text without specialist help before 1990 when cheaper laser printers and desktop publishing programs allowed users to combine word-processed files with digitised graphical information. Before then the technician could have used one of the more restricted ranges of fonts available on a dot matrix printer. Ten years before that the message would probably have been typed, perhaps by a secretary, without 'saving' the text and with little choice of typeface.

Activity

One way of understanding how this text has been made is to word process it (font Courier 10), and then alter it until it is like the original. If you do this you will see the writer has made a number of choices about the text's appearance. What are they?

Commentary

Some of the text is centred, and some of it is aligned on the left-hand side. The writer has also made choices about bullet points, which were not possible on a typewriter, and he has made a distinctive choice about font, and changes the size of it too. The unusual choice of font signals the dramatic import of the message: the typeface is an imitation of the kind of stencilled writing painted on to twentieth-century military equipment and has the **connotations** of jeeps, guns and dangerous life-threatening situations. Control of the font enables the writer to deviate from the conventional expectations of official notices with their authoritative typefaces.

The text also seems to combine features of speech and writing in a way that is typical of documents made with new technologies and their 'home-made' production contexts. The layout blocks the text out into sections but seems to alternate between marking the text grammatically to show how it is constructed, and prosodically to show how it should be read out. The punctuation and line length control the way the text is read. The top two lines function as an attention-getting title and con-textualising sub-title. Then the text style changes, and starts a complex sentence with an if/then structure implied by the words 'If when' at the start. This is interrupted on the next line by another change in font size for emphasis. 'Stop' is also a focus word, both grammatically in its unusual end of sentence placing, and graphologically by being centred with four suspension points on either side. The convention for suspension points is usually three dots in a row, and their effect can vary from acknowledging deleted text, to indicating passing time. Here they seem to serve a prosodic function by indicating a pause for emphasis; so making the text more like something spoken. The two bullet points are in a grammatically ambiguous relationship because of the punctuation and sentence boundary marking. The opening sentence could be punctuated to finish at the end of the first bullet point but because it is part of a graphically matched pair of imperative sentences it could also end with 'Stop'. It is not clear which choice is intended.

Grammatically, the text is forceful; the sentences take an **imperative** form with the two declaratives both giving informational warnings (your work is at risk). This strident tone is complemented by the **pseudo-prosodic features** suggested by the use of graphical devices such as capitals and emboldened letters. These contribute to the illusion of a text being spoken: it 'shouts' graphically in the capital letters and emboldening of 'Virus Alert', 'Stop', 'NOT', and the final two (unpunctuated) sentences. The e-mail convention by which capitals indicate shouting may also confirm this sense of a strident tone.

The composer of this text has used the new technology inventively in a number of ways not constrained by the conventions of traditional formal institutional notices. He has enhanced the appearance and presentational impact of the text as a paper-based poster. The computer gives the writer control over aspects of layout, discourse, **prosodic** punctuation and tenor, which would not be available as easily with a typewriter, or by handwriting.

Cyborg graphology and punctuation

In the last unit there was a discussion about how ICT texts can constrain their users by making demands about the means by which data must be 'inputted'. In particular, there is the demand that information is keyboarded, often in plain text and symbols. In the next text, an e-mail screentext, the writer has much less control over the appearance of the page. All the text is in a plain font and much of the layout is driven by computer protocols over which the user has little control.

18

How much is this text driven by computer protocols? List specific features of both content and layout which tell us that this text is an e-mail.

Text: E-mail forwarded message

```
Date:        Tue, 13 Apr 1999 05:15:36 -0400
From:        CD <CD@compuserve.com>
Subject:     FW: this is a very dangerous virus, much worse than "Melissa",
Sender:      CD <CD@compuserve.com>
To:          "SH" <SH@demon.co.uk>
             "CL" <388000.9975@compuserve.com>
             "MM" <GroupSolutions@compuserve.com>
X-MIME-Autoconverted: from quoted-printable to 8bit by mail.stbrn.ac.uk id KAA07383


----Original Message----
From:        AC
Sent:        Monday, April 12, 199 7:36 PM
To:          'CD'
Cc:          'LM'; 'AC'; 'IH'
Subject:     FW: this is a very dangerous virus, much worse than "Melissa",

Hi, I received this virus warning today - it is useful to read the message
as it looks nasty. Anne

> ----Original Message----
> From:      INTERNET: GP@northbritish.co.uk
> Sent:      12 April 1999 13:51
> To:        ChangeNavigators
> Subject:   FW: this is a very dangerous virus, much worse than "Melissa",

-------------------Forwarded by GP/NORTHBRITISH/on 12/04/99 11:23------------------------

>> AG <agreene@demon.co.uk> on 12/04/99 9:43
>> To:        LS <LS@highlands.com>, AW@rw946.gov.uk, GP <GP@northbritish.co.uk>,
>> PH <peter@tpm.org.uk>
>> Subject: FW: this is a very dangerous virus, much worse than "Melissa",

>> We have been asked by our IT department to alert people to this virus – you may already
>> know about it.
>> Alison

>>> ----Original Message----
>>> From:      GP
>>> Sent:      12 April 1999 09.04
>>> To:        AG
>>> Subject:   this is a very dangerous virus, much worse than "Melissa",

>>> WARNING
>>> If you receive an email titled "Be Happy" DO NOT OPEN IT. It will erase everything
>>> on your hard drive. This is a very dangerous virus, much worse than "Melissa", and there
>>> is no remedy for it at this time. Pass this warning along to EVERYONE in your address
>>> book.
```

Commentary

In this sequence of e-mails each text is embedded within the next, and also comments on it, giving the text some of the properties of an unfolding dialogue or a classroom note. Much of it consists of machine-generated standard headers which record the electronic addresses and identities of the addresser and addressee, the date and time the message was sent, the subject, and whether the information is a copy (shown by (fwd)) or original.

The addresses include the @ symbol, which is a most distinctive and common electronic punctuation feature. It is a Querty and ASCII feature which previously used to function as a sign for retailers' pricing (e.g. four dozen gloves @ £4.00 a pair). It now precedes an electronic address and functions for both a human audience and as a piece of machine-readable syntax.[5] Similarly, the use of the greater than/less than arrows frames the addresses and the greater than symbol indicates a copied e-mail. In all these cases the graphological devices are as much for the computer's electronic reading of the text as for human communication needs.

Perhaps because of the constraints of the plain text format and the keyboarded words there are also a number of features of new CMC graphology and punctuation, which have a human rather than computer audience and allow the communicator to show nuances of meaning,[6] display their electronic literacy skills and their capacity to customise the standard keyboard-constrained interface. Keyboard-based text symbols are used to create pseudo-prosodic effects: the kind of effects that speakers create by non-verbal communication and the paralanguage of volume, pitch and intonation. The most well known of these include capitalisation to indicate shouting, asterisks to indicate emphasis and smileys and similar emoticons to suggest the stance and disposition of the writer and how the reader should interpret the message. The placing of 'burners-on' or 'flame' in brackets before a statement may indicate that a message has been composed in haste and its angry tone should not be taken too seriously, as in the following example where the writer acknowledges her annoyance and aggressive tone with bracketed asides.

Ordinarily, I'd say . . . [FLAME MODE ON.] But I think perhaps . . . yes.

[SCALD MODE ON.]

Very well. Make a cup of coffee. Measure it with an actual thermometer. God only knows how you're preparing it to get it up to 90 degrees C to begin with – preheating the grounds with a blowtorch . . .[7]

20

It has been suggested that the use of 'burners-on' type constructions in business contexts came about to avoid e-mailers causing offence accidentally by loosing off their ill-considered messages. The relative ease with which a message can be composed and sent, and the tendency to use a direct conversational style, along with the absence of the inhibition which might come about from concern with a person's face-to-face response, led to e-mailers writing messages that were too direct and face-threatening. The burners-on framed the message and softened its impact.[8]

Animating words in multi-modal texts

A third aspect of ICT graphology is the animation and networking of linked texts and media in hypertext documents such as webpages. This creates a number of distinctively new opportunities allowing control of how words appear, disappear, move, change colour and size, or trigger other words, media or texts. Sequencing and movement can be used to constrain the order in which something is read and the pace of reading. Text can be highlighted by colour, movement, or association with other moving graphics. Colour may indicate 'live links' that can trigger movement on to new texts. The reader/user may be invited to interact with the text in simulated dialogue. In the process the words may acquire some of the **paralinguistic** properties associated with speech. However the semantics of the written text may be pushed into the margin, being only one of the means of signification available.

This has enabled new modes of linked discourse and new ways of evaluating texts – the latter often themed around notions of convenience and useability. Ease of use, 'intuitive' design elegance, interactivity and navigability are all terms and concepts used to assess web design, and none of them appear focused on the words, meaning and content of a site. Web pages that consist mainly of word processed pages are dismissed in such phrases as 'shovelware'.

Summary

This unit has suggested some of the ways in which new communication technology gives writers access to new multi-modal ways of presenting information in which the verbal is complemented by the graphical (layout), auditory (sounds), kinaesthetic (moving text) and organisational (hypertext links). Such texts may embed information with an electronic status such as the @ sign. Some technology texts include

21

pseudo-prosodic features to create semantic nuances that comment on how the text should be read.

Extension

1   Redesign the Virus Alert text using another font and different spaceshifting to change its impact. Type the text into a screensaver like Marquee on Windows and adjust the font style, size and speed until your text has the impact you want. You may have to shorten the text slightly to do this. Which words and phrases would you edit out, and why? What advantages does this animated screensaver notice have over its paper text equivalent?

2   Websites are commonly assessed for multi-modal features such as design, ease of navigation and interactivity. Investigate a number of newspaper and magazine reviews of websites in relation to their http subjects. Then look at the websites in question. Make a table recording how the screentext differs in its properties from a print equivalent. For example, look at how the text is sequenced and paced, and consider the effects of this.

3   Escape the constraints of the keyboard. Carry out an investigation of Internet punctuation including smileys and emoticons. Build a database of different symbols and their meanings and their functions. Then interview a sample of your peers to see who actually uses them, why and in which genres: e-mail, Internet chat, bulletin boards or discussion groups.

4   Investigate the use of graphological devices to indicate structure in a web page or hypertext document. What devices and conventions can you find and what functions do these serve?

5   Investigate the use of punctuation and other graphological devices in comparable texts from the 1960s and the 1980s. Is there any evidence of changing patterns? For example, are bullet points taking over from semi-colons?

Selling IT – how new technologies are represented

This unit outlines some patterns in the representation of communi-cation technology in advertising and other media texts. It notes patterns to be found and relates these to theories about the movement towards more informal ways of communicating in public, the mixing of infor-mational and persuasive language for marketing purposes and the way that the commercial pressures influence the ways in which new communication technology is presented. A key idea is the way in-animate technology is personified and presented as human, friendly and often business-focused.

> Q: What's the difference between a used car salesman and a com-puter salesman?
> A: The used car salesman knows when he's lying.
>
>   (Anon., quoted by Ted Nelson)

Technology does not exist in a vacuum but in the web of human choices, relationships and power; broader social changes will impact upon the way it is represented and developed. Kress[1] has given the analogy of gun-powder, invented by the Chinese and used for centuries for festive fireworks before coming to the West and being used immediately for aggressive military purposes. Many of the new communication

23

technologies discussed in this book were developed initially for business purposes in the context of a globalisation and a world market economy and the pressures from this have shaped the way the technology has been presented and developed.[2] In particular, the representation of technology often mixes informative and persuasive purposes and is notably informal in the relationship it seeks to strike up with its reader or user.

In these respects the representation of computers is typical of broader social changes identified by linguists such as Fairclough[3] and Kress who have argued that the language used in public and institutional contexts is changing and that styles of private language have crossed borders into public situations in a new style of public colloquial address. The **informalisation** of style and the mixing of persuasion and information for marketing purposes (**marketisation**) can be applied to both the representation of computers in media coverage and in software documentation such as program guides, help files and CBT tutorials.

Advermation

The newspapers and magazines that keep us abreast of technological development are also dependent on advertising revenue, particularly to fund IT supplements and specialist magazines; it may not be surprising therefore that information and persuasion are frequently mixed together in upbeat, enthusiastic accounts about how buying Widget 2000 will solve this or that problem. Coverage of imminent computer developments is characterised by wild claims about the effect computers in themselves will have on human 'productivity' and often personify the electronic and inanimate as a human agent co-worker with qualities of speed, power and diligence. A rudimentary grammar checker is marketed as 'the easiest way to improve your writing' without objection, a politician makes the dramatic claim that 'investing in computers will catapult schools into a high tech future' and there is frequent collocation of computers with words such as revolution, progress and education.

Informalisation and marketisation

The phrase 'public colloquial'[4] has been used to refer to the use of informal language associated with private contexts of friendship in public, government and business communication. Informalisation, as its name suggests, is about styles that suggest an easy-going social relationship between writer and reader. This is based upon informal address terms, direct address to the reader with the second-person pronoun (you), casual colloquial expressions of a type associated with everyday colloquial speech between friends and a relative lack of formal politeness markers.

Related to informalisation is marketisation or the tendency towards advermation where the giving of information is bound up with selling in a market place. Thus Fairclough discusses the ways in which self-advertisement and selling the reputation of the department has crept into the kinds of text generated by Higher Education lecturers. Claims made in such discourse may relate to desirable aspects which encourage purchase, recruitment or financially oriented behaviour as much as the dissemination of information.

In texts about computers there is frequently a tension between neutral descriptive content such as technical specifications and more dramatic persuasive uses of language to dramatise the inert and make it accessible to the reader.

The descriptive language uses a rhetoric of numbers applied to complex specialist terminology and it may well not be understood by less technically informed readers. Because of the speed of technical development, a 'scorching' Widget 350 may be sluggishly obsolete two years later.

Information may be dramatised and made more vivid by being combined with evaluative adverbs (fully), comparative and superlative forms (faster, hottest) and metaphoric language about power, heat and speed.

Another common approach is to personify it by ascribing it human attributes. The technical term for this is anthropomorphism: 'attributing a human feature to anything irrational or impersonal'. Anthropomorphism can take casual forms to make electronic process more easy to understand. For example: 'the protocol handler got confused' or the program 'is trying to do something'. It can also lead to dramatic extended comparisons as in the following examples.

Activity

Look closely at the following pages from marketing leaflets, and identify how they set out to flatter the intended reader. Look at the dramatic claims made about the computer and observe some of the patterns of words, meanings and imagery in the light of the ideas above.

Text: Advermation: Dell sales literature

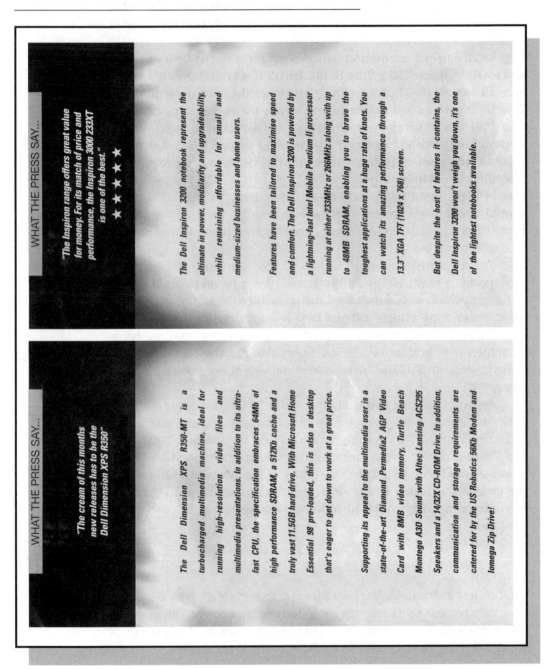

WHAT THE PRESS SAY...

"The Inspiron range offers great value for money. For its match of price and performance, the Inspiron 3000 233XT is one of the best."

★ ★ ★ ★ ★

The Dell Inspiron 3200 notebook represent the ultimate in power, modularity and upgradeability, while remaining affordable for small and medium-sized businesses and home users.

Features have been tailored to maximise speed and comfort. The Dell Inspiron 3200 is powered by a lightning-fast Intel Mobile Pentium II processor running at either 233MHz or 266MHz along with up to 48MB SDRAM, enabling you to brave the toughest applications at a huge rate of knots. You can watch its amazing performance through a 13.3" XGA TFT (1024 x 768) screen.

But despite the host of features it contains, the Dell Inspiron 3200 won't weigh you down, it's one of the lightest notebooks available.

WHAT THE PRESS SAY...

"The cream of this months new releases has to be the Dell Dimension XPS R350"

The Dell Dimension XPS R350-MT is a turbocharged multimedia machine, ideal for running high-resolution video files and multimedia presentations. In addition to its ultra-fast CPU, the specification embraces 64Mb of high performance SDRAM, a 512Kb cache and a truly vast 11.5GB hard drive. With Microsoft Home Essential 98 pre-loaded, this is also a desktop that's eager to get down to work at a great price.

Supporting its appeal to the multimedia user is a state-of-the-art Diamond Permedia2 AGP Video Card with 8MB video memory, Turtle Beach Montego A3D Sound with Altec Lansing ACS295 Speakers and a 14/32X CD-ROM Drive. In addition, communication and storage requirements are catered for by the US Robotics 56Kb Modem and Iomega Zip Drive!

26

The more obvious patterns include the implied personification of the computer as a willing employee, 'impatient ' and 'eager to get down to work' (and at a good price). There are references to speed and power with another implied comparison: this time to a tough vehicle with an intrepid driver at the wheel ('enabling you to brave the toughest applications at a huge rate of knots'). There are persistent references to number and to abbreviated forms of specialised language that presuppose high levels of technical knowledge on the part of the reader. The tough and heroic, performance-obsessed and technically knowledgeable **narratee**/buyer appears to be a business user who is not only impressively aware of these complex specifications but also money-minded and concerned to get a good deal. This tricky customer is also someone who wants ease of use, and not to be weighed down. Fortunately they can find this ease by watching 'amazing performance' through a 13.3 XGA TFT screen.

Other features of the language include its direct address ('you'), and punctuation and vocabulary features suggesting a spoken mode ('and what's more') and an excited tone (the exclamation mark). There is also a suggestion of informality in the idioms, phrases and clichés of informal spoken language: 'well taken care of', 'on board' and the pun on the physical and psychological meanings of 'weigh you down'.

Read through the following computer review and think about the extent to which you feel included or excluded by the vocabulary. Draw up a list of the technical words and phrases you don't understand. Then list the features of persuasive language, including language of claim and evaluation.

27

Text: Advermation: software review

Software Library

● **Essential Utilities**

Adobe Acrobat Reader 3 (Win 3.1/95)
The free Adobe Acrobat Reader lets you view, navigate, and print PDF files across all major computing platforms. (Fully functioning reader.)

GIF Construction Set 1.0Q (Win 3.1/95)
The quickest and most professional way to create transparent, interlaced and animated gif files for web pages. (30-day shareware.)

DirectX 5.0 (Win 95)
Set of essential video and audio drivers that are required to run some of today's processor-hungry games and applications. (Fully functioning drivers.)

Graphics Workshop 1.1Y (Win 3.1/95)
Graphics Workshop is a superlative image management package that allows you to view, convert and catalogue your images in a wide variety of formats. (30-day shareware.)

Graphics Workshop Patch (Win 3.1/95)
Patch file to update Graphics Workshop to the latest version.

Microsoft Internet Explorer 4.0 (Win 3.1/95)
Surf the internet with the latest versions of Microsoft's Internet Explorer for Windows 3.1, and 95. (Fully functioning unregistered version.)

MIRC 5.31 (Win 3.1/95)
Provides a user-friendly interface for use with the Internet Relay Chat network. The IRC network is a virtual meeting place where people from all over the world can meet and talk. (30-day shareware.)

Paint Shop Pro 3.11/4.14 (Win 3.1/95)
Fully-featured painting and image-manipulation program. Features include powerful painting tools, photo retouching, image enhancement functions, batch file format conversion, and support for over 30 different file formats. (30-day shareware.)

SpellWrite for Windows 1.6/2.1 (Win 3.1/95)
A unique utility that can spell-check any Windows program instantly (e.g. email, accounts, database etc.) from a designated hot key. It has an 85,000-word dictionary in UK format. (30-day shareware).

WinZip SR 6.3 SR-1 (Win 3.1/95)
Industry-standard compression/decompression utility for Windows 3.1 & 95 with automatic built-in disk spanning support for multi-disk Zip files. (21-day evaluation version.)

● **New This Month**

Avery Wizard 1.0 (Win 3.1/95)
Makes printing onto labels, cards and indexes easier than ever before. It takes you through a series of simple on-screen steps and templates for formatting and printing 64 different Avery products. (Full version.)

BugCollector Pro 2.0 (Win 95)
BugCollector is ideal for software development teams, helpdesk staff, quality assurance, and anyone who needs to know the status of your software's error reports and feature requests. (30-day trial version.)

Cribator 2 (Win 3.1/95)
Cribator allows you to create, edit and store texts and programs on a PC and to send them to an HP 48G calculator. (Evaluation version.)

CriSP 5.1 (Win 95)
A powerful yet easy-to-use cross-platform file editor. Suitable for programming, writing HTML for web pages, or to manipulate very large data files. (45-day trial version.)

Eraser 1.0 beta (Win 95)
Enables you to erase a file by wiping its contents beyond recovery, scrambling its name and dates and finally deleting it. Fast, secure and very flexible. (Shareware.)

HotSlots 1 (Win 95)
3D Hotslots is a multi-featured slot machine game with real-time 3D animation and colour graphics. (Function-limited demo: reduced features.)

Commentary

This text seems to have a friendly inviting tone, pitching itself intimately if intrusively to the reader with the second-person pronoun in 'lets you'. There is a pattern of evaluative language which makes claims 'essential', 'all major', 'fully', 'unique', sometimes using superlative constructions 'quickest and most professional'. There is a use of particular technical language including specialist words and phrases made up of words in specialist collocations (multi-disk Zip files, fully functioning reader). A number of the technical terms are compound words and it is possible to guess something about the nature of the terms from the headword and from the words that describe it (the **pre-modifiers**). Some of these words and phrases are very technical and specific in their reference and only make blurred sense to a non-specialist: 'drivers', 'disk spanning support'. Many have a metaphoric nature, which embodies an electronic process into a concrete image: 'spanning' and 'processor hungry'. Others are more problematic. For example, what does the phrase 'fully functioning' mean?

As with the previous text, complex information is combined with informal social relationships that lighten its burden on the reader.

Eliza and the chatterbots

In the previous texts the human is projected on to the machine, but many IT texts show the process in reverse with attempts made to design computers to simulate human language behaviour. Much of the increased computer processing power of recent years has been dedicated to improve the user-friendliness of the technology by improving the ways the interface simulates human to human communication .

In extreme, there is the programming of software 'bots' to behave as if they are human interlocutors in interactive written discourse. So Eliza, a computer built by Joseph Weizenbaum in 1966[5], was designed to simulate pyschoanalytical therapy by reformulating operator answers to keep a conversation going. Weisenbaum was 'startled to see how very deeply people conversing with [the program] became emotionally involved with the computer and how unequivocally they anthropomorphised it'. He gave the example of his secretary starting to converse with it and asking him to leave the room after only a few interchanges.

29

Activity

Read through this extract of a dialogue between an Eliza chatterbot and Australian writer G.C. Beaton and identify the successful exchanges (or adjacency pairs) and the stranger turns. How do you think Eliza works out how to respond to Beaton's turns, and which give 'her' most difficulty and why?

Text: Turing Test dialogue

ME: I'm worried about the future.

ELIZA: How long have you been worried about the future?

ME: Since was I was a teenager & I heard about the greenhouse effect & the ozone layer.

(ELIZA interpreted this answer to be: "I want it to be that way forever" ??)

ELIZA: Why do you want it to be that way forever?

ME: I didn't say I wanted it to be that way forever – I said I'd been worried about the future since I was a teenager.

ELIZA: Why do you tell me you were a teenager just now?

ME: Because that's how long the future has been worrying me.

ELIZA: Do any other reasons not come to mind?

ME: My teenage years were crucial to me – they shaped the way I think/respond/worry.

ELIZA: Why do you say your teenage years was crucial to you they shaped the way you think respond worry?

ME: Because I want to come to grips with my worry & fears about the future.

ELIZA: Why do you say your worry fears about the future?

ME: ELIZA – I want to be optimistic about the future – or if I can't be optimistic – then at least I don't want to be depressed by my pessimism.

ELIZA: Do you wish that you can't be optimistic then at least you don't want to be depressed by your pessimism?

ME: That's right ELIZA – I don't want to worry – if the world is going to end in some environmental conflagration or if all humans are going to be supplanted by cyborgs then at least I want to be cheerful about it – like other people.

ELIZA: What resemblance do you see?

Does your computer have mood swings?

More fanciful anthropomorphism can be found in literary treatments. Computers, in spite of being inanimate, can generate peculiar feelings of loyalty and personal affiliation. Part of this may be in the simulation of the confidant: the habitual close relationship they have in composition processes such as writing. For example, consider this extract from McGrath's *Hard, Wet and Soft* when the narrator returns from months spent away from her computer.

> Returning to the Apple Mac after all this time, I feel as though I'm stripping off in front of a parent. It has seen me change from the person I was to the person I am. It has felt the sting of my first disillusionment. But of course we are both proud and neither of us is prepared to admit that things are not the same. The machine displays the same prompt screen it always has displayed and gives no hint that anything is different. As for me, I move through the same almost unconscious list of commands.[6]

Activity

In a similar vein, Magnus Linklater makes a humorous extended comparison between a failing long-standing computer and a death in the family. Read through the passage and consider how he combines vocabulary, imagery and specialist language from the human and computer contexts.

31

Text: Anthropomorphism: The day my computer died

There has been a death in the family this week. As so often in these matters, it has been a slow and painful one. But in this case there has been an extra dimension to the grief: the departed one has taken valuable secrets to the grave, information which may never now be recovered. Our dearly beloved computer, its origins betrayed by the copyright sign Microsoft 1987, has gone to the great database in the sky.

The signs came early on. Starting up each morning was an increasing struggle. The terrible warning sign 'Disc Boot Failure' appeared ever more frequently on the screen, followed by wheezing sounds from somewhere inside the frame as we tried desperately to encourage it to face another day. A gentle touch to the starter switch produced the best results, but we found it helpful to leave it for ten minutes or so while it gathered its strength to try again.

We called in a computer medic who looked it over, somewhat unsympathetically we thought. He suggested that it was malingering. What it really needed, he said, was a sharp blow to the side of the monitor, and he gave it one. So shocked was the machine that it did, indeed, spring into action and proceeded to boot up, download and print out with a speed and accuracy it hadn't managed in weeks. But later it was clearly drained by the activity, and it never again responded in quite the same way.

Finally the day came when the medic took us on one side and suggested that the time had come to put it to rest and replace it with a brand-new machine. He was clearly no great believer in the need for grief-counselling and seemed to us rather more enthusiastic about extolling the virtues of the new MS-Dos 6.22 model with Windows and increased-megabyte-capacity than he was in easing the departure of our friend and companion. But he did stress that it would be kinder all round if we accepted the inevitable. We held a quiet family conference and agreed it was for the best.

There is a rather harrowing ritual involved in disposing of a terminally sick computer. One has to extract any remaining files contained on its hard disk before handing it over to the dealers to do what they have to do. I decided that this should be carried out at the shop rather than subject the family to the pain of actually seeing it happen. I therefore unplugged it for the last time, loaded it into the back of the car and drove quickly away without telling anyone.

I am not, I confess, very brave about these things. I simply left it with them, told them to do whatever was necessary, and then let me know the result. The telephone call, when it came, was worse than I could possibly have imagined. They had opened up the outer casing, but had found that the hard disk was so badly corrupted that they couldn't extract the files remaining on it. The machine was being kept alive only by some electronic life-support system. I was shocked to the core. I heard myself saying: 'I demand a second opinion.' Then: 'Don't move, I'm coming round.'

I leapt into the car and raced to the shop. The sight I saw was too awful for words. There, wired up to a series of other machines, its screen barely flickering, was my computer. I scarcely recognised it. The outer casing had been removed and its insides were revealed: a row of electrodes, wafers and chips, the bits you don't ever want to know about.

'Was there anything important on it?' said the computer man. 'Important?' I yelped. Only every single letter I had typed and stored over the past five years, a veritable cornucopia of correspondence, a time capsule of communication. If I lost that I lost half a decade of my most intimate life. True, there were also some of the most boring letters ever written, but there were others which, well. . . . I asked if I could at least read some of the filenames. Just seeing them brought tears to the eyes.

I leant over the familiar keyboard and whispered some encouraging words. Then I moved the cursor onto the top file and pressed Enter. For a moment I thought I heard an answering groan, then the screen sputtered out: Error reading Drive C. Abort? Retry? Ignore?

It was a terrible choice for anyone to make, worse if you were consigning part of yourself to limbo. I pressed Retry, but I knew in my heart it was no good. The computer man murmured something about a London specialist with a brand-new treatment. Expensive of course, but possibly worth a try. I shook my head sadly. It would just prolong the agony.

We both knew what had to be done. He raised a final questioning eyebrow and I nodded. Then he switched it off.

Summary

From this unit you should be clear about some of the language features that characterise computer coverage in the media and particularly the notion of informalisation. You will also be aware of the concept of anthropomorphising technology to make it simulate the human and the way this figures in advertising, literary treatments and in software interactions with users.

Extension

1   Over the past fifteen years there have been changes to the documentation that accompanies computer hardware and software. Collect some examples from different periods over the past fifteen years. What patterns can you see in how it has developed? Look out for and identify language patterns which lead to informalisation and marketisation and the simulation of human communication.

2   Investigate examples of the anthropomorphisation of technology in contrasting registers. For example, look at the use of such features as greetings, address terms, use of questions, politeness markers and modal verbs in grammar checkers and other computer software simulating human interaction.

3   Research the linguistic features of computer 'chatterbot' interaction by carrying out a library and Internet search for the '**Turing Test**', 'Eliza' and other 'chatterbot' sites. Familiarise yourself with how these work, download some sample exchanges and compare these with transcripts of face-to-face communication. Start with http://kingston.ac.uk/users/k967325/eliza.htm and then look at Plant[7] and the netting-it.com site.

4   Look at the Eliza archive of more successful and convincing psychotherapy session conversations listed under the link 'Eliza was an early computer program' or on G.C. Beaton's website. Why do you think these work better? Then try out some chat with Eliza yourself. What observations can you make about the language of bot dialogue? You can get into Beaton's site and get further guidance for this activity via netting-it.com

Specialising in IT – jargons and subcultures

Aims of this unit

This unit looks at the specialist language surrounding information and communication technology and asks what purposes it serves and for which groups. It introduces ideas about how language can function for reference, in order to get things done, and as social plumage, to show individual and group identity.

There is a distinction to be made between jargon for instrumental technical purposes and jargon for social purposes. One linguist, M.A.K. Halliday,[1] has suggested that it is possible to consider language in relation to three overarching functions, or metafunctions:

1   ideational – concerned with representing ideas;
2   interpersonal – focused on sustaining relationships;
3   textual – which helps the larger units of meaning to cohere in text or discourse.

Specialised reference and semantic field

Specialised activity inevitably creates the need for an associated specialised language to refer to it. Many new technology words refer to the new entities made possible by technical development. For example, the units of measurement like **byte** and **baud** have a technological and physical basis as measurements for electronic information transfer and storage. Such terms can be a means of being precise and explicit; they can also exclude people who don't share that language. In his book on jargon, Walter Nash[2] refers to such language as shoptalk or 'the phraseology of pursuits' and sees it as 'inevitable and enriching' in contrast to 'show talk' or 'the aping of flashy words and phrases' and sales talk 'which pleads acceptance for some kind of product' by a language that 'precludes free analysis of any proposition'.

There is a fine dividing line between jargon in the sense of 'unintelligible language', and jargon in the sense of 'a mode of speech familiar only to a group or profession'. The newness of technology can create contexts where people have very uneven access to it and a word can act like a **shibboleth** showing membership of the group. This can happen just through the resentments that come from not understanding what is being said.

Activity

Look at the following passage and consider the effect of this language on the intended users and on the general reader. Then read through the technician's e-mail discussion on page 84. To what extent do you feel included by this language and what purposes does it serve for those using it?

ROB (to MARC): Have you transferred the video?
MARC: Uh huh, to AVI flc format.
ROB: Run Photomorph to Windows.
MARC: I think I got it going.
ROB: What d'you capture?
LOUIS: Is this LST OK?
MARC: I left C3K here.
ROB: Did you do the full spread or just part?
LOUIS: Off the TV?
MARC: Yeah but I haven't checked it yet.
ROB: Open her up, then.

MARC clicks on a file icon and a crudely pixellated video grab recorded from the TV appears. An advertisement for sanitary towels . . .[3]

Commentary

The specialist terms used by the technicians act as specialised shorthand for them as they mix computer protocols and human language in a bizarre mixed register; they also exclude the general reader. The banal focus for their action, the sanitary towel advertisement, makes their esoteric knowledge and specialised references seem absurd and self-important, as the writer intends by this juxtaposition.

Jargon for exclusion

The use of new words can be deliberately socially orientated as in the following extract from the same novel where a character is excluded because she has used the wrong form of a word (the diminutive and over-familiar 'nettie' instead of 'nethead'), though neither term is one with a technical meaning.

> 'What about a wool modem?' asks Helen. Jenny loses her smile.
> 'No, no, no, that really wouldn't look right.'
> Jenny tosses her crop and addresses herself to Helen:
> 'Trust me, you're talking to a Nettie here.'
> Helen and I swap glances and the smallest of titters.
> 'Nethead,' says Helen politely.[4]

Like Nash, computer enthusiasts differentiate between different types of exclusive language used by them. The Introduction to *The New Hackers' Dictionary*[5] categorises three different types of hacker jargon.

1   Hacker slang: from mainstream English and not technical sub-cultures (e.g. user).
2   Hacker jargon: slang language peculiar to hackers.
3   Techspeak: the formal technical vocabulary of computer science as found in textbooks, technical dictionaries and standard forms.

Activity

Look at the following vocabulary list of Net language. Look again at the different ideas about the purposes of specialist language on the previous pages. How would you classify the purposes of the words in this list? How many of these words are there for technical reference and how may for social purposes?

Text: Net language

Shorthand: Net acronyms

It doesn't take long in IRC to realize that Net acronyms are peppered with the F-initial. It's your choice whether you add to this situation, but if you don't tell people to 'f*** right off' in ordinary speech or letters, then FRO is hardly appropriate on the Net, and nor is it adding F as emphasis. However, you may at least want to know what's being said. And, BTW (by the way), the odd bit of Net shorthand may be useful and/or vaguely amusing, even if unlikely to make you ROTFL (roll on the floor laughing).

AFAIK	As far as I know
AOLer	AOL member (often not a compliment)
A/S/L	Age/Sex/Location
BOHICA	Bend over here it comes again
BBL	Be back later
BD or BFD	Big deal
BFN	Bye for now
BRB	Be right back
BTW	By the way
CUL8R or L8R	See you later
CYA	See ya
F2F (32S)	Face to face (skin to skin)
FB	Furrowed brow
FWIW	For what it's worth
GDM3	G'day mate
GRD	Grinning, running, and ducking
GR8	Great
HTH	Hope this helps
IMHO	In my humble opinion
IYSWIM	If you see what I mean
IAE	In any event
IOW	In other words
LOL	Laughing out loud
NRN	No reply necessary
NW or NFW	No way
OIC	Oh I see
OTOH	On the other hand
PBT	Pay back time
RTM or RTFM	Read the manual
SOL	Sooner or later
TTYL	Talk to you later
YL/YM	Young lady/young man
YMMV	Your mileage may vary
|LY| & +LY	Absolutely and positively

Smileys and emoticons

Back in the old days, it was common in Usenet to temper a potentially contentious remark with <grins> tacked on to the end in much the way way that a dog wags its tail to show it's harmless. But that wasn't enough for the Californian E-generation, whose trademark smiley icon became the 1980s peace sign. From the same honed minds that discovered 71077345 inverted spelled Greenpeace's *bête noire*, came the ASCII smiley. This time, instead of turning it upside-down, you had to look at it sideways to see a smiling face. An expression that words, supposedly, fail to convey. Well, at least in such limited space. Inevitably this grew into a whole family of emoticons (emotional icons).

The odd smiley may have its place in diffusing barbs, but whether you employ any of the other emoticons in use is up to your perception of the line between cute and dorky. All the same, don't lose sight of the fact that they're only meant to be fun :-). Anyway, that's up to you, so here goes:

:-)	Smiling	:-L~	Drooling
:-D	Laughing	:-P	Sticking out tongue
:-o	Shock	(hmm)000.:-)	Thinking happy thoughts
:-(	Frowning		
:'-(	Crying	(hmm)000.:-(	Thinking sad thoughts
:-)	Winking		
X=	Fingers crossed	0:-)	Angel
=)		}:>	Devil
{}	Hugging	(_)	Beer
:-*	Kissing	:8)	Pig
$-)	Greedy	\o/	Hallelujah
X-)	I see nothing	@}`-,-'--	A rose
:-X	I'll say nothing	8:)3)=	Happy girl

A few others, mostly Japanese anime-derived, work right way up:

@^.^@	blushing	^_^;	sweating
*^_^*	huge dazzling grin	T_T	major tears

If you still want more, try consulting a few unofficial dictionaries on the Web. Use "smiley dictionary" or "emoticon" as a search term at http://www.hotbot.com

Commentary

It would have been reasonable to guess that some of these Net **acronyms** would have had a technical **referent**; acronymy is associated with shortened versions of the long compound words that characterise technical jargon. In fact nearly all these words appear to be about maintaining social relationships and striking social stances. Some of them may also have a textual function in marking topic boundaries or closing the conversation down.

Anti-language and covert prestige

Halliday also developed a theory for understanding the insider language used by marginal or oppositional groups. Using examples from accounts of language from three subcultures separated in time and space (Elizabethan vagrants' speech, Calcutta gangsters and Polish prisoners), he suggested that such marginalised groups can create a specialist vocabulary which is as much concerned with social purposes as specialised reference. Such groups will tend to **re-lexicalise** words by inventing new terms or re-using words for new meanings. There may also be a process of **over-lexicalisation** in which there will be more words than are necessary for communicating the specialised meaning. So, for example, in street culture there may be far more colloquial words for cannabis than are required for reference. This abundance of terms will typically show patterns of metaphor, humour and insider references. They may show the need to have specialist words for particular types of specific activity. There may also be patterns of system and logic.

In some respects computer jargon shows features of anti-language particularly in the codes of hacker morphology. The tone of much of the language shows humorous, metaphoric and extreme **taboo**-breaking choices. The pattern is there in the origins of **spamming** and **boot-strapping**. Other examples include joke initialisms such as IRL/RL for in real life and the acronym TWAIN – said to stand for 'thing with an interesting name' and the repetitious use of F and the F-word in acronyms. All this might imply oppositional, subcultural values and possibly, given the research on swearing and gender, a male identity. Another feature of the language is elaborate overstatement as in the acronyms ROTFL and ROTFLOL (rolling on the floor laughing out loud). These words with their taboo-breaking behaviours and metaphorical references function as shibboleths creating a group identity for the users which defines their own shared social ties and excludes those outside the group.

Nerds, anoraks and newbies

There is also a popular stereotyping of people with expertise and enthusiasm for communication technology. Newspaper and magazine journalists routinely stereotype computer enthusiasts as dysfunctional, de-socialised, one-trick dogs who are probably young unattached males. Whilst this is often done in a humorous vein, it seems to reflect widespread derisive popular social attitudes. Terms such as **nerds**, **geeks** and **anoraks** proliferate to the extent that a computer search of a newspaper from 1996 showed that anorak was used in its pejorative sense about people (as an abuse term for a technophile) more commonly than as a term for a fashion-obsolete garment. At a time when racist and sexist language behaviour is condemned in most people's private attitudes and is proscribed officially by equal opportunities policies in institutions and by legal statute, it is strange that there appears to be very little critical comment about these attitudes.

Extension

1   Investigating technophobia: investigate the pejorative use of a technophobe term such as 'anorak' or 'geek' across a range of texts to determine some patterns in the collocates and situational occurrences of the word. You could consider the following: a variety of dictionaries, CD-ROM newspapers, other electronic reference materials, online magazines, a raw Internet search for the word with a sampling method. The BNC Sampler Corpus (1989–94) has three citations of anorak, all in the literal sense. Can you find any patterns? For example, is anorak more likely to occur in computer contexts than other specialisms? Are there other vogue words associated with it and does it co-occur with the modern colloquial meaning of sad as contemptible? The *Oxford Dictionary of New Words*[6] cites propeller head as another synonym for an over-enthusiastic specialist. Is there any evidence to suggest this word is dying out?

2   Subcultural language: investigate the language of a particular specialist group of new technology users such as game players or a Usenet group. Make a list of the insider vocabulary items and interview members of the group about why they use these words, what they mean, where they learned them, whether the words change. In particular, try to find out whether the words are needed for specialist reference or for style reasons. Then check the words

39

against a dictionary of new words. Which of them are recognised? See if you can search the net or other electronic reference materials to provide some examples of the word in use. For example, at present there is no reference to 'cheat', 'platform game', 'level', 'beat 'em up' or 'point 'n' click'. Extend this activity by providing a definition of one of the words and some citations (examples of use) and writing to a dictionary publisher such as the Oxford University Press. Alternatively you could provide a different sense to an existing word – such as 'glitch'.

3   Investigate the purposes of a new subcultural language. Look at some examples of new language in, for example, a lexical list, a computer magazine article or an excerpt of Internet relay chat and attempt to classify the terms using Halliday's classification system. Is it too simple to say that BTW and IMHO have a textual function to mark topic boundaries, that words such as 'newbie' are at least as much about maintaining social relationships as they are about reference?

4   Read Halliday's account of anti-language and then research hacker language on the net. How helpful do you find Halliday's ideas in explaining hacker morphology? Start with the summary of the jargon file http://www.citysun.ac.uk/acer/slang.htm and go on to look at http://memes.org/jargon/jarginfo.html

5   It is often said that computer language is masculine in origin and orientation and that hackers are mostly men. Examine the taboo-breaking and male oriented language in hacker files. You could start with an Internet search on 'Trojan Horses' and such file names as 'Back Orifice'.

Naming IT – how new words enter the language

Aims of this unit

This unit and the next one are about vocabulary change, or changes in the lexicon (word stock). Vocabulary change is commonly understood as a matter of new words for new things but it also shows both a social and a linguistic dimension. From the social perspective, vocabulary will emerge out of particular contexts of relationships, intentions, communities and power. Considering word origins and how words come into the language can be a productive way of seeing this social dimension and the ways in which new words reflect and define how people are thinking and relating to each other, as well as to the technology being used. Linguistically, words will show patterns of word formation, which relate to patterns in the language. The volume of technology-related language change is such that nearly all types of word formation are there, along with some new varieties (see Unit 6).

Activity

Look at the following lexical list and categorise the words into those with a specialist, technical reference (e.g. 'Archie') and those referring to the social practices of online communication (such as 'newbie') and any which relate to both. What other patterns do you notice?

41

Text: Internet jargonbuster

Internet jargon buster

JARGON seems to be inescapable in the computer age, and nowhere is it more rampant than on the Internet. There are three types that you will encounter. They are tech-speak, acronyms and smileys. Here at The Sunday Times we understand your concerns and have designed this handy 'jargon buster' to help you find your way through it. Keep it next to your PC.

Tech-speak

Archie
An Internet resource for finding files online

Attachment
A program, picture or sound that is sent with an e-mail message

Browser
The software you use to 'surf' the World Wide Web

Flame
To insult or vent your spleen

Gopher
A menu-based information-retrieval system

HTML
HyperText Mark-up Language (HTML) is the programming language of the Web

Lurker
A lurker reads messages but never writes any

Mosaic
The original leading-edge Web browser

Netscape
The new leading-edge Web browser (see next page)

Newbie
A newcomer to the Internet, often used derogatively

Newsgroup
A Usenet discussion group

PGP
Pretty Good Privacy (PGP) is a programme that encodes your e-mail so that only the intended recipient can decode and read it

PoP
A Point of Presence is the place where your local Internet access is based. It determines your phone bill

Sig
A signature file attached to e-mail or Usenet messages, long Sigs are frowned upon

Snail mail
The online fraternity likes to call land-based postal services by this name

Spamming
The universally despised practice of sending junk mail to many different Usenet Newsgroups simultaneously

URL
The Uniform Resource Locator used to address World Wide Web resources

Usenet
A collection of more than 15,000 online conferences accessible via the Internet

UUencode
A method of converting binary files (such as pictures or sounds) into a text-based message that can be sent by e-mail or posted to Usenet

Winsock
A file that enables Windows applications to talk to the Internet, often a source of technical problems

Acronyms

AFAICT As Far As I Can Tell
AFAIK As Far As I Know
AIUI As I Understand It
BTW By The Way
F2F Face to Face
FAQ Frequently Asked Question
FWIW For What It's Worth
FYI For Your Information
IMHO In My Humble Opinion
ISP Internet Service Provider
ISTM It Seems To Me
ROFL Rolls On Floor Laughing
RTFM Read The Friendly Manual
TIA Thanks In Advance
TPTB The Powers That Be
TVM Thanks Very Much
YHM! You Have Mail

Smileys

Remember to view them sideways on

The main four smileys are:
:) Happy
:-(Sad
:-< Frowning
;-) Winking

Other Smileys you may just find useful:
'-) Crying
>:-) Evil grin
:-D Laughing
:-O Shocked
<-O Yawning

Totally useless smiley
B-) Batman
5-) Elvis
8-) Gorilla

Commentary

Well over half of the words in this list are about technical referents and the explanations of the words also include words and phrases that would need their own glossary to be understood by many people. There are also a number of words implying a social focus including 'tech-speak', 'lurker', 'newbie' and 'snail mail'. None of these words is needed in order to use technology, but rather the words carry social attitudes towards technology and its uses. So 'newbie' is a kind of technological innocent implying their powerlessness and lack of access to electronic literacy, and thus suggesting the power and knowledge of the speaker able to evaluate from that stance. 'Lurker' conveys an image of a stalker or voyeur and implies hostility towards an intrusive outsider. 'Snail mail' is a playful synonym for the regular post and highlights its slowness, thus implying the superiority of the electronic alternative.

Where the words come from

Very few words are coinages unrelated to other words[1] and so most have origins and a lexical genealogy. Etymology is the study of those origins or the 'process of tracing out and describing the elements of a word with their modifications of form and sense'.[2] The volume of new technology-associated words entering the language gives an opportunity to examine etymology in action. In looking at them it is possible to see competing discourses between producer-initiated language change, and the language which emerges out of the subcultural groups mentioned in Unit 4. Producers, manufacturers and advertisers label products often using impressive polysyllabic or compound words to draw attention to their special features. This is the language which predominates in advertising and computer specifications. But there is also an informal, idiomatic, colloquial language used by the subcultural groups such as hackers and related groups. This leads to expressions marked by humour, metaphor, colloquial style, concrete imagery and abbreviations for economy.

Linguistic recycling

Early horseless carriages were built with a buggy whip socket. Today's simulated paper is comparable.

(Ted Nelson, *Computer Lib*)

43

New technology vocabulary sometimes has language 'fossils' in which a term from a past technology is recycled in other but related ways. For example, 'dashboard' used to refer to a board which stopped the stones from horses' feet hitting the carriage and its occupants, and then came to refer to a partition between a vehicle engine and its passengers. This new word doesn't exist in isolation but close to other words in new contexts of use and in different registers of language, so the **collocations** may well be different. The new uses will encode a different range of cultural attitudes and this may bring new connotations. In the process of changing to a vehicle interior feature, the emphasis, the properties and the collocations of dashboard may have been affected by car marketing and its new everyday use: dashboard may be associated with car styling, dials, controls and gauges, rather than as a raw physical obstruction to oil, noise and filth. Many words and phrases used about new technology are older words used in quite new ways. This is true of much of the language of word processing, which refers to a paper technology of documents, files and wastepaper baskets.

Activity

Even in a small text such as the Virus Alert notice (see p. 16), there will be words and phrases which would have seemed new or unfamiliar in 1970 and which won't be found in many dictionaries. Look through the text again and make a list of any words which you think might have been developed since 1960. Look out for technical or field-specific lexis. Additionally, try running the text through a computer spellchecker.

Commentary

You might be surprised to find that there is only one completely new word: 'reboot'. Even this word is not entirely new: we can see a recognisable prefix 're-' and the familiar word 'boot', and so we can infer that this is a related word; 're-' implying some repeat process. It is the same word form and spelling but the referent it refers to is entirely different.

According to the *Oxford Dictionary of New Words* 'reboot' has very little to do with the original word but relates to a **clipping** from a specialist metaphoric expression 'bootstrapping': an idiomatic image referring to the way the computer pulls itself up by it bootstraps when it starts, programming itself with a sequence of instructions which allow it to function. Bootstrapping is thought to have been an allusion to a character in the adventures of Baron Munchausen who pulls himself up by his bootstraps. The word was in use in the 1980s and early 1990s at a time when computer use called for more expertise and technical understanding than is the case now, and where the social groups using computers were more of a specialist subculture. According to the *Encarta World Dictionary* the word featured in a software programme called bootstrap loader and was extended into the phrasal verb 'to boot up'.

As is common with the language for technological change, an elaborate metaphoric image for a new process led to a word which was then clipped in the interests of verbal economy and flexibility (rebootstrapping). It is also a word with its origin in a specialist subcultural group, which has then gone into wider circulation, and into a context where its etymological meaning may not be understood. 'Spam', in the sense of mass postings of electronic junkmail, is a similar and better-known example of this new type of word which has its origin in a cultural allusion.

---

spam /spam/ *noun* and *verb* Also written **Spam**

noun: In online jargon, the undesirable practice of posting the same message repeatedly to a large number of Usenet newsgroups.

intransitive verb: To post a spam.

A figurative use of the trade name of a US brand of tinned meat (see below).

The world-wide Usenet system (see NET) consists of many thousands of subject-based discussion forums called NEWSGROUPS. It is improbable that any widely-disseminated message could be relevant everywhere it appears and the usual reason for **spamming** is to advertise, which is a grave breach of online custom. In the US the word spam became associated with the practice through the highly-repetitious *Monty Python* restaurant sketch, in which *Spam* appears to be served with everything:

> Don't make a fuss, dear. I'll have your spam. I love it. I'm having spam spam spam spam spam spam spam baked beans spam spam spam and spam!

The term reached a wider public in April 1994: two US lawyers aroused great controversy when they posted a message to thousands of newsgroups to advertise their services in obtaining Green Cards (US immigration permits); other *spams* are the 'Make Money Fast' chain-letter scam and the advertising by a New York legal firm of their credit-renewal services. The person who *spams* is a **spammer**. The offence is strictly so called only if the message is individually posted to each newsgroup instead of being *cross-posted* (cross-referenced so users only have to download it once); if it is cross-posted, but to excess, the usual term is *velveeta* (named after a US brand of processed cheese).

> What the Arizona lawyers did that fateful April day was to 'Spam' the Net, a colorful bit of Internet jargon meant to evoke the effect of dropping a can of Spam into a fan and filling the surrounding space with meat . . . And all over the world, Internet users responded spontaneously to answering the Spammers with angry electronic mail messages called 'flames'. Within minutes, the flames – filled with unprintable epithets – began pouring into Canter and Siegel's Internet mailbox.
>
> — *Time* 25 July 1994, p. 51

> The alt.current-events.net-abuse Usenet newsgroup is the place to discuss spamming and other obnoxious advertising.
>
> — *Everybody's Internet Update* Feb. 1995, online newsletter

---

Figure 5.1 Definition of spam

How new words come into the language

Knowing the etymology of a word, such as the existence of a meta-phorical allusion to Baron Munchausen or to Monty Python, doesn't explain its journey from inception to widespread recognition. Linguists have identified four idealised stages in this process (see the figure below) starting with 'potential', or the need for a word; 'implementation', including early instances of this word in private or restricted, specialist contexts; 'lexical diffusion', referring to its wider spread through the language; and 'codification', in which a word achieves an official status by being recorded in dictionaries, spellcheckers and other authoritative records of usage. At the stage of lexical diffusion the word may start to be used in a prestigious written source such as a newspaper. To see this illustrated dramatically research the origin of 'Oscar' in the *OED2* CD-ROM.

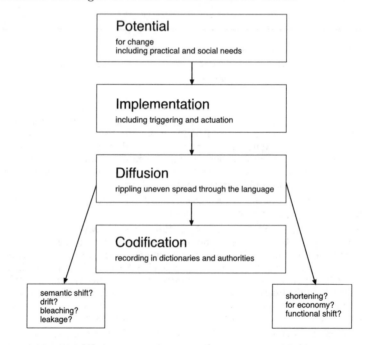

Figure 5.2 Lexical change flow chart

Loanwords and metaphorical extension

New words can 'be borrowed from the existing word stock by semantic shifts, which create a new unit of meaning within the word reference' (Algeo 1999). This has happened with the words 'virus' for a destructive computer program, and 'hack' for gaining illegal access to computer files.

Such changes are common in new technology language. For example, the Virus Alert text includes only one new word ('reboot'), but there are several instances of old words being used for new meanings: 'virus', 'floppy', 'disk', 'drive', 'alarm'. The shifts in meaning are often metaphoric. This can help clarify and make more vivid the ideas and concepts. New technology processes can be complicated, technical and abstract, so providing imagery for the invisible processes helps audiences understand what is going on. For example, a computer virus is a program which alters and deletes files without the instruction of the computer user. It can be moved electronically by being stored on a disk or by being transmitted down a network cable. It is like a virus because it is independent, destructive and it can spread, and it brings with it a kind of language spread of associated terms from its medical imagery: disks can become infected, your work can be 'at risk' and an anti-virus program may be described as a 'disinfectant', or it may be even be a 'Doctor'. This virus image is only one of the many examples of invisible, abstract computer processes being described metaphorically in concrete terms, and bringing with them a raft of related imagery and associations.

The word 'disk' refers to the 'circular storage media used in computers, CD players and other recent technology' (floppy disk, compact disk). It has come to us from American English, as we can see from the spelling. The American English spelling is a useful indicator for British English readers that the disk is of a type associated with new technology. The spelling marks it out as a separate word. For American readers it would be a semantic widening of an existing word. Something similar can be found in the case of the word 'program', which was the American English spelling of the word spelt 'programme' in British English. This has a specific new technology meaning in UK English, but is a widening of the word 'program' in US English. In both cases, these are loan words in British English, but arise out of semantic widening in American English.

Word origins can reveal the significant underlying powers in a culture. Historical accounts of language change sometimes emphasise the importance of military and political force, for example in the dramatic disappearance of written Old English in records for the two hundred years that followed the Norman invasion of Anglo-Saxon England; but now economic dominance is likely to be more important. 'Disk' and 'program' typify the influence of the USA: much of the technology was first developed and used there and so it picks up its language in that place of origin. The words are then disseminated along with the spread of technology. Some linguists have raised concerns about new technology leading to a cultural imperialism which privileges English and especially American English over other languages. The process is not universally welcomed. The French Academy has tried to restrict the use of English terms including those for new technologies, and has offered French language equivalents for technical innovations, with only limited success.[3]

The global context of new technologies blurs the traditional distinctions between loan words and **semantic widening**. English words may well have been loaned from US English.

Technologies developed in other countries may still be expressed in English because of the status of English as the preferred language of the global market. For example, 'Walkman' is made up of English vocabulary, but was a product name used by Sony which became used as a generic term.[4] The use of product names as generic terms is another fairly rare source of new lexical items: 'hoover' for vacuum cleaner, or even 'PC', which originally referred to IBM Personal Computer.

Who started it?

A number of linguists have drawn attention to the difficulty of identifying actuation, or the initiation of change. In new communication technologies particular individuals and social and economic groups have sometimes had an unusual degree of identified power in this process although a question is then how a word has come to be taken up and used by others.

The word 'hypertext' was conceptualised and formulated by Ted Nelson in the 1960s. Nelson has said that he was very deliberate in his choice of words and justifies the use of hyperspace in mathematics as an analogy. However, as he admits, the word did not become widely known and used until over twenty years later.

> But suddenly in 1986 the idea caught on. It may have been the notecards program from Xerox.... It may have been Gary Kildall's opening speech at the 1986 CD-ROM conference; it may have been the appearance of the Hypertext Guide program from Owl in Seattle, and possibly as the result of commercial development, computer software manufacturers began using it [the Hypertext Guide program] in the 1980s.[5]

Similarly, according to the *OED* the original etymology of multimedia relates to the presentation of educational materials, and not necessarily new technology. Hypertext seems to have become a more popular word once the Internet became a mass commodity because it is a way of referring to the organisation of text rather than its material form.

Other words coined by Nelson at the same time have not become generic terms: for example 'hypermedia', by which Nelson meant something like a technological fusion of hypertext and multi-media, appears to be infrequent. 'Docuverse', for a world-scale set of linked texts, remains a specialist term. Nelson also commented on the failure of his word 'text handling', which was replaced by the IBM term 'word processing'. He has argued that text handling is a better description of the referent we now know as word processing, and the new word was political because 'word processing' fitted in with a particular suite of dictation product names IBM was marketing at the time (1969).

The success or otherwise of Nelson's coinages is revealing about the importance of commercial development in the spread of new vocabulary. Again, the language of ICT is bound up in the marketing decisions of multinational companies. The traditional distinctions between generic terms, **hyponym** subcategories, and product names have been replaced by a number of competing discourses which may be market-driven, and contested. The appropriateness of the terms may well give way to the realities of economic power.

As is well known, the novelist William Gibson in his novel *Neuromancer* first used 'cyberspace' and 'virtual reality' in 1984. Gibson also makes repeated reference to 'the matrix', an idea that seems like a future developed Internet.

> Case was twenty-four. At twenty-two, he'd been a cowboy rustler, one of the best in the Sprawl. He'd been trained by the best, by McCoy Pauley and Bobby Quine, legends in the biz. He'd operated on an almost permanent adrenaline high, a byproduct of youth and proficiency, jacked into a custom cyberspace deck that projected his disembodied consciousness into the consensual hallucination that was the matrix. A thief, he'd worked for other wealthier thieves, employers who provided the exotic software required to penetrate the bright walls of corporate systems, opening windows into rich fields of data.[6]

These words are relatively unusual because we know the circumstances and the individuals concerned. Interestingly, they are all compound words. More often a word will arise out of a community in unpublished forms, so the trace is less obvious.

Other coinages have become world standard although their origin may be in unnamed specialist communities, and it may be very difficult to get further than speculation. The influence of big commercial power

49

has to be set against the power of computer-literate subcultural communities. Mark Dery has written about the links between 1960s' drug culture, surfers and the 1980s' computer subcultures. For example, 'surfing' as a verb for using the web, may have had its origins in the US West Coast and groups which were characterised by counter-culture attitudes and a love of computers as a tool for individual freedom. Surfing may be making an implied analogy with West Coast surfer culture.[7] *The Oxford Dictionary of New Words* gives a very different word origin relating it to the vogue for expressions such as 'trainsurfing' and 'channel surfing'. Whatever the origin, the word was not popularised until the 1990s when the web became technologically accessible. The word now functions metaphorically as part of the marketing discourse of 'the net'.

The computer bytes back

Words and phrases once focused on the computer domain are now applied to other contexts and the word's meaning widens to more general reference. This process is known as semantic widening or **leakage**. For example, the expression 'user-friendly' is often associated with computers and new technologies but it can have a wider reference.

Activity

Take a look at this **KWIC list** from *The Times* for the word 'user-friendly' in 1996 and note the contexts in which the word is used here. Is there a dominant context? Are there any contexts which you find new or surprising?

Text: KWIC list of user-friendly

```
               USERxFRIENDLY: 45 entries (sort: 5L,5L)
N                              Concordance
1      the concept abhors, here  was a very user-friendly sort of introduction to t
2  ing 404 and still an inviting, intimate, user-friendly space. The show is bas
3          NVQs and making the system more user-friendly. It offers some sensible
4       6s PCs be made more palatable and user-friendly to the general consume
5         have been refined to become more user-friendly,&#148; says Jack. Most
6     come less of a castle and more of a user-friendly palace. An &#147intelli
7  ll the changes in working patterns, a user-friendly office needn &#146t be
8      fort in Dell&#146s approach: forget user-friendly; it must be positively us
9  puter champion, illustrates, in super, user-friendly colour graphics, the we
10   parents cope with computers. It runs user-friendly reviews of computer pr
11  we are trying to do is make things as user-friendly as possible to take out
12   public examinations. None will be as user-friendly as these. They have be
13  tuck to examples like this, with some user-friendly illustrations, North woul
14  tuck to examples like this, with some user-friendly illustrations, North woul
15      Features John O&#146Leary on the user-friendly first stage, carefully de
16   ally the NHS, in mind are now more user-friendly. The NHJS wants wheel
17    ed, mostly in America. They all have user-friendly databases and video gr
18  first step in making the lottery more user-friendly &#148. He added that t
19 inistic. But it is expected that a more user-friendly mixture of hormones fo
20      kitchen and were consequently non user-friendly. Yours sincerely, Jim L
```

Commentary

This is an extract from three pages of KWIC lists generated from a year's copies of *The Times*. Over 80 per cent of the instances of user-friendly were collocated with computer references. A search of a CD volume of the *New Scientist* between 1989 and 1996 generated 120 hits in 57 articles. Looking through a sample of those shows approximately 80 per cent with computer collocates and contexts but the exceptions show the beginnings of the leakage of the word into other domains, as in the following comparative form: doctors' surgeries are becoming user-friendlier.

Summary

This unit should have helped you to understand some of the processes by which a word comes into the language and the gap between word origins and wide-scale recognition.

Extension

Investigate the etymologies of the following words: Flame, smiley, boot, surfing, net. See the website for guidance on information sources.

Forming IT – how new words are structured

Aims of this unit

This unit looks at word formation, or morphology, to see some of the patterns in the way new technology words are made. In their word formation, spelling and pronunciation, new words are likely to be constrained by the lexis, phonology[1] and grammar of the language: for example, it would be hard to have a word like 'cgsxhewltd', which would not fit with existing patterns of consonants, vowels, morpheme shapes, or spellings. Linguists have developed a taxonomy or system for classifying types of word formation and the volume of new technical words coming into the language is an opportunity to see these classifications in action; it is also possible that there are some interesting differences in patterns of some of these new words.

Patterns in new technology

According to Crystal[2] there are a number of common processes for word formation including the following, which have been illustrated by examples from new technology words:

affixation	rebooting, resetting, debugging, Megadrive
backformation	wordprocess (verb) from word processor

compounding	cyberspace, hard disk drive, CD-ROM, desktop, laptop
conversion	floppy (noun), access (verb), video (verb)
acronym	RAM (random access memory)
initialism	SGML (standard general mark-up language)
blending	**netiquette**, internaut
clipping	disk, floppy, video (noun and verb)

John Algeo, in the *Cambridge History of English Language*, develops a classification system for word formation based on four factors: whether the word has an etymon (word element) based on earlier words, whether the word omits any part of an etymon, whether a word combines two etyma, and whether any of the etyma are from another language. He uses six groupings: creations, shifts, shortenings, composites, **blends** and loans. The schema is shown in Figure 6.1.

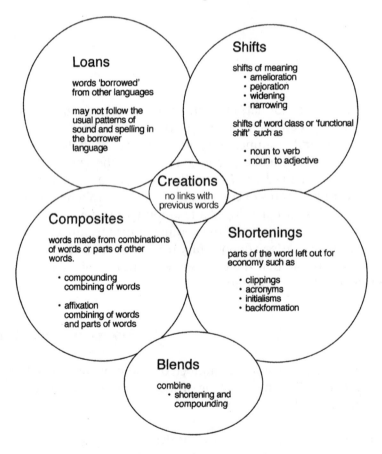

Figure 6.1 Schema for word formation types

Algeo gives a table showing the different percentages for types of word formation in a set of samples taken from different dictionaries. This is interesting for demonstrating the importance of composites, and especially compounds, over other types of word formation. Shifts and shortenings are also important, with very few creations, blends or loan words. His scholarship can be summarised as shown in Figure 6.2.

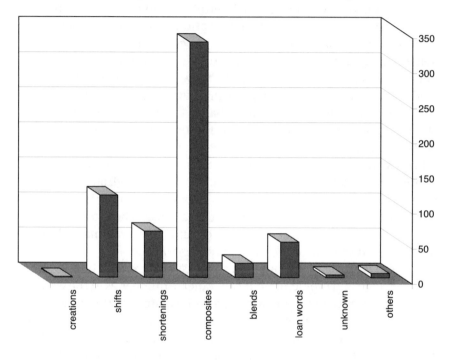

Figure 6.2 Frequency of types of word formation

Activity

Do the words which come into the language with ICT follow this distribution of types? Are there any factors which make particular types of words more likely? For example, are compound words more likely? How often do these get shortened forms? Are there patterns to these shortened forms? See extension activities on p. 62.

55

Affixation

In the case of affixation a word is joined by a morpheme, which alters its sense. As the examples show, often the morpheme is a prefix, or a kind of bound morpheme, which comes at the start of the word. Morphemes are the smallest meaningful chunks into which you can divide a word; so for example affixation combines 'affix' (verb) and 'ation' (bound morpheme) to make the noun. This is called derivational or creative morphology because a new word is derived in the process. Similarly {re}{boot}{ing}, {re}{set(t)}{ing}, and {de}{bug(g)}{ing} can be broken down into the morphemes indicated by the brackets. In these cases a new word has been made because of the meaning of the prefix morphemes, 're' (repeat) and 'de' (more like an antonym), which change the original word. {Set(t)}{ing} etc.: the inner bracket indicates an additional consonant which is there because of a spelling convention in English which associates long vowel sounds with medial single consonants and short vowel sounds with double consonants. It is not significant morphologically. The morphemes at the ends of the words are suffixes, which show the grammatical relationships of number and tense. These are called inflectional or grammatical morphemes and give grammatical information about the role of the word in the sentence.

Mega is also used as a prefix in a process of affixation, but this word is more recent and problematic. It can indicate number, as in the wartime measurement megaton – where the prefix indicates one thousand (tons). It has come to be used more loosely to indicate high number and quality, and in the process some of the specific meaning has been '**bleached**'. The case of Megadrive, a product name, may be an example of vogue affixation, where a word is placed in front of another for image as much as for reference. As Jean Aitchison[3] has explained, this happened with the word mini, which became popular in the 1960s. Mega also has a vogue slang meaning in which it functions as a free morpheme with the meaning 'extreme'.

Compounding

Compounding refers to the process where two or more words, or free morphemes, are placed together to make a compound word, e.g. hard disk drive, CD-ROM, cordless mouse. This has always been a very common feature of new technology terms, which show a tendency towards lego-like combinations of words (agglomerations) in compounds, portmanteaus and blends: video recorder, television, netiquette.

Traditionally Latin and Greek etyma have featured in such hybrid combinations as 'tele-' (from afar) 'vision'/'phone' (see/speak). A compound usually has a headword which often occurs at the end of the word. This acts as the focus for the previous word(s) that function like modifiers. So a 'hard disk drive' is a type of drive, and a 'cordless mouse' is a type of mouse. The example of 'CD-ROM' is more complex, as we shall see below.

This agglomerating process allows for complex classifications and categorisations within the field of science and technical innovation. For example, a 'floppy drive' can be distinguished from a 'hard drive' which can be distinguished from a 'CD-ROM drive', which can be distinguished from a 'zip drive', and so on. As this example shows, compounding allows for the creation of **hypernym** and hyponym relationships and for quite complicated models of categorisation. 'Drive' describes the function within the computer, and the first word shows the type of storage. This complexity will only have a force of specific meaning if the audience has the technical knowledge to understand the distinctions. For that audience such compounds will be an economic way of encoding complex information. It has been observed that in noun compounds there can be a number of different meaning relationships between the parts. For example Bauer contrasts 'tetanus jab' (A is prevented by B) with 'flu virus' (A is caused by B).[4] Using his semantic classification system, you may find that (A is made of B) and (A is part of B) are dominant types of compound.

The *Oxford Dictionary of New Words* reports the use of the word 'ware' as being a particularly productive combining form in the making of composites for types of computer terms: so 'software', 'shareware', 'nag ware' (shareware which nags you to register), 'bloatware' (overspecified programs). It also draws attention to the use of compounds linked by a full stop such as 'net.god' and 'net.users'. This construction is 'unique to computer networking' and alludes to the use of a full stop as a delimiter in computer programming. Both these types of compound appear to be informal and subcultural in origin, showing the influence of small cohesive groups and the rapid diffusion of such words in the language of new technologies. More recently 'e-' has been a popular combining form as in 'E-commerce' for electronic commerce or the backformed 'E-tail' for electronic retail.

Such language would make sense to a technologically informed reader. For others the language may seem mysteriously complex, and long-winded, and this may in turn give rise to verbal strategies which simplify or replace the jargon in the interests of verbal economy.

Compounding in product names can provide particular scope for advertisers: at the impressionistic level it can make the product seem impressively technical, and gives an economic means of noting key aspects of specification.

Compounds can be left as individual words, hyphenated, or even pushed together without hyphenation. The lack of agreement in the conventions used by different publications is an example of language undergoing change before standardisation. Typically, you might expect a new compound to be left as separate words and for later developments in hyphenation to give way to a single word.

Functional shift

Functional shift, also known as grammatical conversion, occurs when a word changes its word class. For example, a noun becomes a verb (fax) or an adjective becomes a noun ('floppy' from the clipping of 'floppy disk'). This seems to be a process for referring to new meanings with economy, but it can affect older words too. English is particularly prone to shifting forms from one part of speech to another because of the relative lack of word endings marking parts of speech, unlike the case system in German or Latin.[5] The ponderously latinate term 'facsimile' to refer to a direct copy was used to refer to an electronic facsimile copy. These were sent and received by facsimile machine, using the language associated with posted letters in such verb phrases as 'send a facsimile/document'. 'Facsimile machine' has been clipped down to 'fax machine', or just 'fax', and the latter can now refer to either the machine or the document. This in turn has spawned the verb 'to fax' as in 'I've faxed a document' or 'sent a fax'. The focus of the word is now on 'faxing' as the electronic process rather than the nature of the text. So the noun 'facsimile' has led to the verb 'fax'. Similarly the noun 'e-mail', itself a compound word which contains the initial 'E' for electronic, can now be used as a verb. In the same way, the computer-associated processes associated with verb phrases such as 'having access to information' have led to 'access' being used as a verb without an auxiliary: she accessed the information files. In all these examples we can see a word changing its word class, and doing this as part of a process which may have involved compounding and clipping.

Backformation

Backformation is where a word loses part of itself to spawn a related word in a different word class. The lost piece of the word has been treated as if it were a morpheme. One well known backformation is the verb 'to burgle' which was formed from 'burglar' (noun) and has replaced the original verb 'to burglarise'. Similarly, the noun 'word processor' to describe the equipment, led to the verb 'to word process'.[6]

Technological innovation and analogy can lead to strange new compounds and phrases of a semantic kind: such as 'print *to* file', and 'softcopy', for screen text as distinct from hardcopy – paper print out.

Acronomy

Initialisms and acronyms take the first letter of each word in a compound word or noun phrase and use these to make a word, e.g. RAM (random access memory) and ROM (read only memory). This allows for a complex set of ideas compressed in a compound to be compressed still further. This can allow for memorability (all acronyms are mnemonics which aid memory) but it may be popular more for phonological economy. The difference between an acronym and an initialism is that an acronym is spoken as a word (scuba: self contained underwater breathing apparatus) and usually written in lower case letters, whereas an initialism is sounded as the letters in sequence (e.g. BBC) and is usually written in capitals and sometimes with full stops between letters. Both word formation processes are ways of being economical in the pronunciation of long compounds and noun phrases. It is interesting that the *OED* gives 1943 as the year in which acronym was first recognised for the Dictionary. This was in the middle of the Second World War and a time when many new technology words for apparatus were coming into the language. There was a need for acronomy in a wartime social context where people were handling complicated technology as a matter of routine. The specific references contained in the long compound expressions did not need to be repeated with every use, and slang insider language may have been a way of expressing specialist knowledge.

Acronomy is governed by the phonological rules of a language. So, for example, an acronym will tend to have a vowel in the middle of consonant clusters. It would be possible to have 'radar' but not 'rrdaa'. Initialisms are free from these constraints.

Initialism

Both initialisms and acronyms are associated with formal technological processes and jargon. However, they can also take the form of keyboard shorthand in interactive written discourse. These contexts can give rise to subcultural language of humorous mock initialism forms such as ROTFL and RTFM ('rolling on the floor laughing' and 'read the f–ing/friendly manual'). These can have a different function to the traditional technical initialisms. ROTFL is a means of animating text with stage directions, whilst RTFM can operate as a shibboleth to put down 'newbies' who show their inexperience of the system and its protocols.

Clipping

Clipping refers to the way in which words are clipped down to shortened forms, e.g. 'morphing'. This is a very common process partly because the original technology words are so long. The desire to be efficient and avoid redundancy leads to words being shortened into acronyms, initialisms and clippings. For example, 'floppy' refers to the soft or floppy portable magnetic disk as distinct from the hard, non-flexible and permanent disk in the computer. Originally these were $5^1/_4$ inches in size and were floppy on the outside and the inside, before being replaced by hard plastic $3^1/_2$ versions. Like many other IT expressions, 'floppy disk' has undergone a process of clipping and disk has often been clipped down to 'floppy', so the modifying adjective has become a noun. Alternatively, people may use the clipped form ' disk', with floppy left out. 'Floppy' may be interpreted by some less technically minded audience as a misnomer because of the hard casing of $3^1/_2$ disks.

Clipping can also give rise to new inflexional suffixes to indicate plurals and so on. This can give rise to unusual letter combinations, such as those found in the plural of the clipping 'video': 'videos'. If you want to find how unusual the text string 'eos' is, try using a computer search on several large documents. It is interesting that this word regularly attracts misspellings such as 'video's' and 'videoes'.

Blending

Blends are words which combine morphemes from two words and imply a blend of meanings of those two words. One famous example is Lewis Carroll's word chortle,[7] which is said to suggest a mix of snorting and chuckling. Blends are an unusual type of new word and catch on through a serendipity of puns and close-sounding words.[8] 'Netiquette' (net + etiquette) is now fairly well established and general. 'Internaut' (astro-naut/inter-net) has been used to describe someone who explores computer communication.

Hacker morphology

In addition to the conventional means of creating words in English identified here, there are types of coded word formation developed by hackers and related subcultural groups. These word formation types are self-consciously logical and based on shibboleths and insider references. They have been described extensively in the Internet jargon file, and this has been summarised by Mike Green.[9] This type of subcultural word formation or 'jargonification' includes distinctive word formation principles including the following, from Green's summary:

Verb doubling	'Mostly he talked about his latest crock. Flame. Flame.'
Soundalike slang	New York Times → New York Slime
The '-P' convention	'State-of the world-P?' Imitation of coding convention
Overgeneralisations	Dubious → dubiosity
Spoken inarticulations	'Mumble' or 'sigh' as stage directions
Anthropomorphisation	'And its poor little brain got confused' (about a program)
Comparatives	Sliding scale evaluations such as the following about code quality: monstrosity, brain-damage, screw, bug, lose, misfeature, crock, kluge, hack, win, feature, elegance, perfection

See netting-it.com for links explaining this in more detail.

Summary

This unit has outlined some of the ways in which ICT words are structured and the linguistic dimensions of morphology, phonology and semantics. It has identified a common tendency for elaborate computer noun phrases to be shortened in use. It has touched on the dynamic which leads to further changes to word structures in shortenings.

Extension

1   According to Algeo, functional shift is encouraged in English because of the relative simplicity of inflexional word endings in nouns, verbs and adjectives. Make a preliminary investigation of the use of a word undergoing functional shift such as a noun becoming a verb. Is there any evidence of a further shortening taking place through clipping, acronomy or some other process of change?

2   Investigate the word formation patterns of an ICT-related word list. Compile a glossary of new technology terms used with computers or with game consoles. See if you can classify these using Crystal's or Algeo's list of different word formation categories or the hacker jargon morphology list. Make up into a table and chart. What are the patterns in the domains of language used? What observations could you make about the levels of formality used?

3   Make a tally of new ICT words in this book or from a source such as the *Oxford Dictionary of New Words*. Then classify the words by the types of word formation described in this chapter. Aim for at least 100 examples. Then transfer the numbers and groupings into a spreadsheet program such as Excel and make up a chart to compare with the norms established by Algeo. To what extent does the chart follow the benchmark proportions established by Figure 6.2 and how would you account for any deviations you find? See netting-it.com for details and templates to use.

seven

Watching IT – tracking new words

Aims of this unit

This unit gives you methods of tracking vocabulary change with the aid of a computer and presenting that information in the way used by lexicographers. It will give you some experience of the kind of work that goes into making a dictionary entry and the problems involved in that work. These methods can be used to track any type of new word and can also be adapted for phrases and other 'text string' patterns of words and letters in combination.

This unit will be more meaningful if you have access to a computer, and some reference CD-ROMs or Internet sites such as newspapers and an electronic version of the *Oxford English Dictionary*. Spend some time familiarising yourself with the structure of a short dictionary entry from the latter.

Bodies of text

So far we have looked at the nature of electronic texts, and the representation of the technology which makes them. There is a third dimension in the capacity of technology to search through data and organise these into information; this is related to the discussion about ASCII text in the first unit. Computers make it possible to join large numbers of texts to develop a body of language, or corpus, that can be searched for statistically significant patterns. For example the British National Corpus (BNC) is 100 million words long, and joins up 4,000 different sources of contrasting language registers: speech, writing, formal, informal, private and public, many of them 40,000 words long. The computer word search facility and the availability of electronic text archives and language corpora make it possible to trace a word and its patterns in its contexts of use, spelling, hyphenation and other details. For example, the BNC can be searched for a word or phrase and in a matter of seconds it will display a KWIC list of all the examples it can find.

The creation and analyses of very large bodies of electronically readable tagged text in language corpuses are part of the sub-discipline called corpus linguistics. There are many other large text databases which are not corpora in the strict sense of a body of texts but which can be revealing about language change. For example, newspapers on CD-ROM and on the Internet record vast amounts of language in a narrower variety of registers. Such papers as *The Times* are seen as authoritative, credible, high status representations of the language, and material is dated. They thus provide some index of the acceptability and frequency of new words. These texts are useful for two reasons: they amass a body of data large enough to reveal patterns and they indicate whether a word is acceptable enough to be in the house style of the newspaper.

The availability of such texts makes it possible to do some interesting first-hand computer-assisted lexicography, tracing words as they come into the language and then developing a provisional account of patterns and movements in their situations of use, meanings and collocates (or co-occurring words). This technique was demonstrated by Professor Jean Aitchison[1] in her technology-assisted investigation of the word 'joyriding', made after receiving a phone call asking her to 'do something about those dreadful journalists who use the word joyriding when they mean car stealing and people killing'. Her method provides a blue-print that can be adapted for other word searches.

Aitchison started by consulting a very simple authority: a computer spell checker. This did not recognise the word, offering 'garotting' and 'gyrating' as suggestions. She went to consult the *OED* on CD-ROM for an authoritative account of the word and found a definition and examples with a different sense of pleasure trip, particularly in aeroplanes. Tracing through the chronologically listed examples of the word in use she discovered that the earliest meaning of 'taking without consent' came from 1970. Having established the reference status of the word, Aitchison then investigated how the word was actually being used in context. Her reference source, *The Times* on CD-ROM, was searched using the wild card (joyrid____) revealing the different word class versions: joyride (verb), joyrider (noun), joyriding (present participle verb and gerund). Examining the different contexts of use there were clear contextual associations of criminality. Regardless of the official dictionary status of the word, there was an implicit consensus about the meaning and appropriate contexts for use. This consensus was so strong that there was even a cliché collocation: 'teenage joyriders'. The word had also leaked into new situational contexts where the figurative use of joyriders indicated inexperienced people with a reckless attitude: 'The Treasury and Bank of England have been behaving like teenage joyriders with a hot car'.[2] This metaphoric use derived from the new sense of the word shows that the latter is now well established and understood – otherwise people wouldn't understand the metaphor.

Activity

Try using Aitchison's methods as shown in Table 7.1 for investigating a possible new word associated with communication technology. Start by looking the words up on a spellchecker and in various dictionaries. Then carry out word searches using electronic versions of newspapers and other reference materials. See if you can build a list of possible citations to use in an amended dictionary entry.

Table 7.1 Approach to tracking language change

Stage	Task
1	Reporting of a use as different or unfamiliar, deviant form.
2	Checking in a spellchecker.
3	Checking in an authoritative dictionary or a range of dictionaries.
4	Searching in text archives including electronic newspapers.
5	Analysis of citations in terms of meaning, situations of use, likely collocates or co-occurring words. KWIC lists can help this process.
6	Looking for signs of 'leakage' where the word is used metaphorically, 'bleaching' where it is used in a way which suggests a loss of specificity or force, semantic widening or narrowing.
7	Number-based searches in varied reference sources to establish statistical frequency of word use.

Source: Aitchison (1994).

Commentary

A search for 'on-line' (1941), 'off-line' (1941), 'download' (1980) and 'play-ability' (1981) showed that they passed the spellchecker test, and they had all been noted by the *Oxford English Dictionary* as coming into the language some time ago. However, their popular frequent use is likely to be much more recent, and in the case of 'playability' the particular sense with reference to computer games is narrower and more specific than that implied by the *OED* entry. The word 'playability' as used by computer games enthusiasts is apparently now giving way to the compound 'game play', which is in the *OED* but hyphenated and with a different sense.

Investigating language in this way opens up questions about what counts as a word in the official dictionary records of the lexicon and which social groups in which activities are entitled to have their words authorised as standard lexical items. 'Game play' may be common enough in a Playstation magazine but if it exists nowhere else is it any more than jargon? 'Innit' used in colloquial speech by London teenagers is recorded in writing because it is in the Corpus of London Teenagers used in research done by Scandinavian linguists and then included in the British National Corpus.[3] It exists in written form but may only be used within a generation and in certain localities. In the UK the colloquial and generation-related semantic shifting of 'sad', away from pitiable and towards pitiful in its pejorative sense, is well known at the level of every-day awareness and written evidence can be found for it in newspapers, but it is not recorded in either the *Oxford English Dictionary* or the *Dictionary of World English*.

Using computers to track words over time

Computer-text based searches make it possible to extend Aitchison's method and do some amateur detective work in tracking language change, particularly as new words come into the language. This can be done by:

- ◎ doing rough counts of incidences of words in different source texts;
- ◎ analysing early citations of new words where they will often be found highlighted by spellcheckers or with layout indicating new and marked forms: inverted commas, capitals and hyphenation are typical clues;
- ◎ looking for collocates and patterns of situational use. Fre-

quency of subsequent use may be some indicator of lexical diffusion particularly when the numbers can be related to several information sources such as a variety of CD-ROM newspapers from different years. KWIC lists and computer-generated patterns of collocates can help this process.

Print dictionaries, because of their nature, cannot record ongoing language change and this shows up in a field like new technology where a word may go from zero incidence to being commonly known in a small number of years. This has happened with a number of Internet and computer-related words which are barely represented in either the BNC, (collected between 1988 and 1994), or the *Oxford English Dictionary* (*OED*2) although they are now well known and frequently used in authoritative texts such as broadsheet newspapers. Computer-assisted approaches can enable users to map the lexical diffusion of a word from specialist registers into more general use.

Figures 7.1 and 7.2 are based on numbers of raw (unanalysed) references to computer-related words over nine years of *New Scientist* and seven years of the *Guardian* and the *Observer*. Both the keyword search tables can be found on the website along with tables for similar searches in *The Times, Financial Times*, BNC and other sources. All these sources show Internet and e-mail related words as existing from the end of the 1980s but growing very rapidly from 1995. It is interesting to note that the Internet access program Mosaic and its successor Netscape

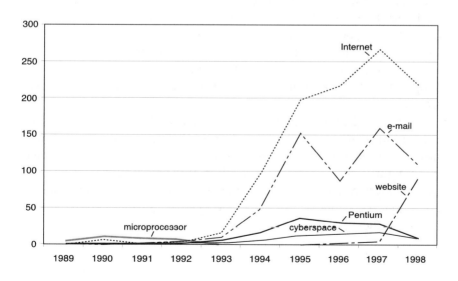

Figure 7.1 Cyberwords in the *New Scientist*, 1989–98

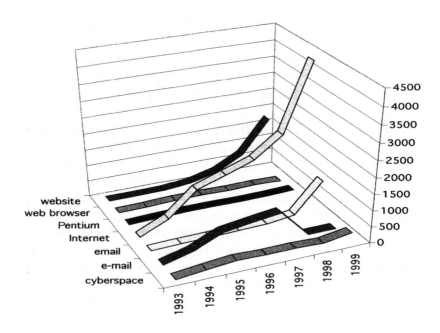

Figure 7.2 Cyberwords in the *Guardian*, 1993–99

Communicator became available at this time: these lowered the technical expertise needed to use the web and made the Internet far more accessible, contributing to rapid mass market development. There is a similarity here with Nelson's comments about the popularisation and diffusion of hypertext in relation to commercial and technical development: indeed, his own 1965 word has achieved immortality since he wrote about the influence of the Guide program because of the adoption of 'hypertext' in the http initialism which appears on every web address.

The English newspaper references seem to indicate a sudden increase in awareness of the terms in mid-1995 from a starting point of near-zero in 1994. As expected, several of the earliest citations of these new words figure first in the more specialised, technologically informed and US-based *New Scientist*. Investigation of electronic versions of specialised computer magazines such as *Wired* and *Byte* might show the curves starting still earlier.

Early citations of Internet words

Looking at the following extract from an article in the *New Scientist* from December 1994 shows how quickly specialist Internet words have mutated and spread into the common vocabulary.

> Every 10 weeks, the number of computers providing information to the World-Wide Web doubles.... The latest figures were collected last month by automated systems that 'surf' the Internet, seeking out the sites that supply information. They show that the Web is growing at roughly 1 per cent a day ... This growth is starting to create problems ... Several people have written programs that seek out Web sites because the task is too time-consuming for a person. But these 'crawlers' can overload Web servers when they access them in order to find out what information they hold, says Martijn Koster, managing director of the networking company Nexor, based in Nottingham. 'There are currently about 20 or 25 robots out there, of which 10 run regularly,' he says. 'About a month ago one hooked onto our Web server and was making so many requests that it over-loaded the machine, which crashed.'[4]

These early citations of Internet words include a number of features which now seem eccentric or laboured, including the use of inverted commas around words now familiar, and words used with a different sense of reference. What we would now know as 'search engines' are then called 'robots', and the early reference to 'surf' is semantically different to its successors: now it is people who are the subjects referred to as 'surfing the net' and not 'automated systems'.

Trying Aitchison's methods, and putting this *New Scientist* article through a spellchecker on Word 95, I noticed the automatic spell-checker's underlining of 'gigabyte' and 'crawlers'. This suggests that none of these words is in the spellchecker. The thesaurus treated 'surf' in its noun sense, and offers this option as a related meaning when the words 'surfed', 'surfs' or 'surfing' are entered. So there is no record of the leisure sense of surf as a verb, let alone the computer field-specific lexeme. This may reflect the business orientation of the program, or restrictions in memory space restricting the database. In other words, the absence from the spellchecker/thesaurus lexicon may indicate the status of a new word, its incomplete assimilation into the language, or it may be revealing something about the bias and implied readership for a computer program.

Looking through a sample of *The Times* from January to June 1995,

69

we can make a number of preliminary observations that could be investigated further. Roughly a third of the articles with references to 'surf' use it in its new computer sense. A small number of articles use surf as a verb with metaphoric function of travelling to somewhere, often to get information. The remainder use the word in its sport sense. There are also some grammatical and metaphorical patterns: the leisure form of surf is often collocated with a preposition with a spatial sense.

Surf to Dundee and pull down data.

Others use 'surf' with 'for' as if it were a synonym for 'search for'. There is some extended metaphoric use of the word .

Surf through the wrong file (File as wave).

Surf is also collocated with ideas of pleasure and self-indulgent enjoyment, sometimes with some striking mixed metaphors.

Surf for the sake of it . . . you can go down wonderful rat holes.

Looking at the list you can also see some graphological variations including a use of inverted commas, and inconsistent capitalisation of the net. Again these may indicate the relatively new and uncertain status of this vocabulary.

The observations would need further investigation to see if the initial patterns were borne out in other materials. Computers and computer databases offer a way of doing this more quickly, but such an investigation would have to show an awareness of the limitations of the database. For example, what would be the implications if many of the surf articles in *The Times*' database had been written by the same journalist who is also a specialist IT correspondent?

Summary

This unit should have given you some methods for analysing language change using computers, bodies of electronic text and simple statistical methods. You will be aware that early citations of words often take a marked form with capitalisation, hyphens or inverted commas.

Extension

1   Use the data and commentary about the language 'joyriding' and 'surfing the net' to put together a simulated dictionary entry for the new sense of 'surf'. If you have access to a computer and to an electronic dictionary such as the *OED*, you could paste a dictionary entry into a text as a template, substituting your material for the original, and deleting the latter as you go. Augment the dictionary entry with other examples taken from magazines, newspapers and advertisements. Can you find any spoken evidence about the word from radio or television? Try recording a topic-related programme and transcribe excerpts where surf is used. Aim to make your dictionary entry as scholarly and authentically presented as possible. Arrange the entry appropriately using fonts to indicate the discourse structure of the entry. Write a brief critique of the strengths and weaknesses of your piece of lexicography.

2   Use the methods outlined to investigate other words. Those associated with new technology can be very productive: Internet, information superhighway, nerd and anorak.

3   Make a statistical analysis of the uses and contexts of a word by finding its uses in several contrasting types of electronic text including dictionaries, newspapers and magazines. Present your information graphically using sample KWIC lists, tables, graphs and a report. What conclusions can you draw about the ways in which the word is being used?

4   Carry out an investigation of compound words in new communication technologies. Using a computer try and see if you can trace the word from early references, with inverted commas or hyphenation, to one-word citations or clippings or other shortened forms.

Picturing IT – mapping meanings on to electronic space

Aims of this unit

This unit is about virtual space: the way that information technology is visualised in extended comparisons and imagery. It introduces ideas about metaphors, symbols and icons and develops the idea of semantic field and relates these to the values and assumptions they imply. Everything we do with a computer is mediated through the language, imagery and metaphors of the interface. What do the choices of such imagery, verbal and pictorial, reveal?

Activity

Look again at the Virus Alert text on p. 16 and identify the patterns of related meanings you can see in the text. List these and then consider the effect of these ideas being put together. Look particularly at collocations, the words that are put together in phrases and compound words.

Commentary

People communicate with each other for purposes and their texts and discourses show patterns of predominant meanings, or **semantic fields**, which indicate the kind of topics in focus and how these are seen. The Virus Alert text comes from a domain of texts about technology and it has a field of technical terms, which were discussed in previous units. There is also a field of danger and damage: virus, alert, alarms, at risk (twice), irrecoverably damaged. There are medical undertones in the use of 'virus' and the medical collocation 'at risk'. This is part of an extended comparison between a destructive computer program and an image of a life threatening condition (at risk, irrecoverably). This set of linked images is supported by a semantic field suggesting urgency of time and due procedure. That is to be found in some of the emphatic adverbials such as 'immediately', 'irrecoverably', and the language expressing conditions and cause: 'if' (twice), followed by imperative structures (If this happens/(do) this). The text fuses semantic fields of computer technology, health damage and urgency to dramatise its content, and communicate more forcefully with its audience.

'Virus' is one of several words that show a metaphoric elaboration where one image is related to others: the extended comparison between the referent and the imagery implies a complex likeness with several dimensions to it. The computer program is dangerous, destructive and infectious. This carries the implication that we must treat it carefully and with due procedure. Such implications are typical of the metaphorical nature of meaning in texts, from the clichés of love as a rose, to the language of battle (campaigns) and games (players) applied to the business 'world' (itself an image).

Metaphors we live by

In their book *Metaphors We Live By*, Lakoff and Johnson argued that metaphor

> is not just a device of the poetic imagination but an everyday practice, which shapes how we think. . . . The concepts that govern our thought are not just matters of the intellect. They also govern our everyday functioning down to the most mundane details. Our concepts structure what we perceive, how we get round the world, and how we relate to other people. Our conceptual system thus plays a central role in defining our everyday realities. If we are right in suggesting that our conceptual system is largely metaphorical, then the way we think, what we experience and what we do is very much a matter of metaphor.[1]

Starting by considering the semantic field of war embedded in the language of argument, they go on to consider the different types of systematic extended metaphor, and their significance. Computer interfaces are rich in such metaphorical systems.

Cultural attitudes to particular areas of human activity can often be seen in the choices of metaphor used when that activity is discussed. Computer interfaces often make references to objects in space and use spatial relationships as a means of making the abstract visual. People 'enter' or 'go' into a program or 'access' a network. Using a program is departure: leaving, quitting or exiting. When stuck in a program you can 'escape'. A complex change of computer systems in a college is described as 'migrating over to'. Furthermore as they 'enter' or 'exit' they are frequently met with the welcomes and goodbyes of IRL behaviour.

Words and icons, bells and whistles

Metaphorical words about space have been replaced by the images themselves, directly manipulated by the user and animated and given **systemasticity** by being part of a virtual environment of extended imagery. The early computer command screens were controlled by typed commands but graphical user interfaces such as Windows replace typed text with imagery, given coherence by the simulation of an office environment. This development, which started with the graphical user interfaces (GUI) introduced in the 1980s, has led to the situation where most computer users know a whole symbolic set or 'iconic grammar' to control their word processor. These symbols have now become so familiar that they appear natural **icons** for their referents. These devices increasingly use some kind of animation: the 'scissors' shut when the user 'cuts', a 'button' pushes in when it is clicked on, file icons can be seen moving through the air as they are 'sent to their destinations'.

Look at a computer running software such as Microsoft Office. Note the systematicity of the office imagery: files, folders, office assistants and wastepaper baskets. Note the consistent and systematic link between computer processes and objects in a physical environment: users open, close and save documents in files, and keep those files in folders, putting them away sometimes in Filing Cabinets. When they get rid of their information they send it to the wastepaper basket or the more environmentally conscious recycle bin.

The strangeness of this parallel universe shows up in the unusual, unfamiliar collocations such as 'Send' to the 'waste paper basket' rather than 'dispose of', 'save documents' instead of 'retaining' them. Also, the office is electronically peopled with strange creatures such as the unseen Wizards and Office Assistants in the form of winking paperclips or cats who offer their help uninvited in response to the moronic mechanisms of pattern-matched code. These bots and macros are governed by the same 'intellisense' of statistical probabilities, algorithms and code that changes my name from *Shortis* to *Shorts*.

The extended metaphor of the business office is a feature of many computer texts and this choice of imagery may be a way for manufacturers and suppliers to relate to their most profitable market: the office, administration and business customer. The extended metaphor is realised both graphically and verbally in the labelled picture icons found in computer programs' graphical user interfaces. It is also realised semantically in the example material provided with 'help files'. These are often written for an implied readership of business executives and marketing managers. This seems to be part of a wider metadiscourse in which a computer is a tool that will earn us all bigger sales and profits and help us become more productive.

Other books in this series have explained the idea of the narratee, or the kind of reader whose interests the text appears to be addressing. We are used to thinking of computer programs such as word processors as 'tools' and mine sits under a folder called 'Productivity'. Programs are also texts and convey social and political assumptions in the choices they offer and in the way they frame those choices. Investigating such patterns in the examples and imagery used in software help files can give an insight into the way the development of ICT has been shaped by the social contexts of informalisation, marketisation and globalisation, covered in Unit 3.

Some early spellcheckers omitted words such as 'ideology', presumably as being irrelevant to the business user. Even now some of the templates offered assume a business function for the document, as in this header for a fax (see Figure 8.1). Note how the design of this structures the user into giving a detailed, explicit data input.

FACSIMILE TRANSMITTAL SHEET

To:	From:
[Click here and type name]	[Click here and type name]

FAX NUMBER:	Date:
[Click here and type fax number]	January 4, 2000

COMPANY:	TOTAL NO. OF PAGES INCLUDING COVER:
[Click here and type company name]	[Click here and type number of pages]

PHONE NUMBER:	SENDER'S REFERENCE NUMBER:
[Click here and type phone number]	[Click here and type reference number]

Re:	YOUR REFERENCE NUMBER:
[Click here and type subject of fax]	[Click here and type reference number]

☐ URGENT   ☐ FOR REVIEW   ☐ PLEASE COMMENT   ☐ PLEASE REPLY

☐ PLEASE RECYCLE

Figure 8.1 Computer program fax template

Metaphorical language change

These metaphorical extensions of the virtual space can be subject to language change patterns in response to design fashions and technical and social change. The template this document 'was written in' was generated by an interactive program called a Wizard. This is also a term used in MUDs and other types of computer gaming subcultures to refer to a person with expert control of software systems who may exclude or otherwise regulate the presence of other players. It is possible that the software world shows a semantic transfer and in its new sense the Wizard is a bot and not a person. Until the early 1990s, it was common to 'park' a hard disk in the drive when turning the computer off (computer as automobile). The Windows interface now tells you that 'it is now safe to turn off your computer', carrying the implication that it would not have been safe before, and that the computer is an authoritative source about its own 'health' (computer as body).

Other mappings of semantic space can be found in the use of

specialist interface words such as 'menu' to describe a restricted set of choices, the 'ruler' for layout, the 'toolbox' for text treatment, the 'palette' in graphics programs. There is similar language about storing information: some compressed files have to be 'unpacked', others can be 'unzipped' (knowledge as substance) and others still may 'spawn' or 'hatch' their own programs (program as unborn being). Similarly, the menu of games' control pads usually includes information about spatial direction, often accompanied by an implied toolbar of weapons. In console games, such as *Tomb Raider*, the verbal and informational rooms of the word processor become graphically realised spaces, with a similar principle that they can only be reached in a certain order unless **'cheat/ jump'** informational links are made. The noise which fax machines make when they are about to connect is called a **'handshake'**.

Studying the Internet shows a pattern of geographical metaphors and value-laden imagery. The geographical metaphors can be seen in the titles of the programs needed to use the net: Netscape Navigator and Internet Explorer. Navigation imagery has been used for some years to refer to reading and making links in hypertext documents. It is extended by such references as 'home', 'go', 'back' and 'forward', and sites are sometimes accompanied by iconic 'arrows' or 'footprints'. In one program, users are invited to 'go for a test drive on the information super-highway', and the helpline is called Members' Assistance, extending the journey metaphor with a vehicle roadside assistance organisation.

Activity

The following is a KWIC list compiled from searching broadsheet newspaper CD-ROMs in 1995 when the Internet was still new. Study this list and note the patterns and groupings that can be made about the metaphorical properties of 'website'.

Text: KWIC list for 'website'

website carries information
constructing a website
withdrawn from its website
dial into the X website
followed on the website
keep a list of visitors to the
    website
links to different parts of the
    website
websites address is
putting up a website
website including collector's
    corner
available free at the website
had they their own websites it
    would bring them closer to the
    people
build a premier website
visit the website
yuckiest website on the Internet
viewing software is available free
    from X website
use it on our website
downloaded from X website
produce a website
woken up to the power of the
    website
rushing to set up a new site
tour this garden sitehopping from
    one website to the next
set up a website
website bristling with Keep Out
    signs
further information on the website
created a website

promoted on a website
find this site of interest
website gives details
provide a new service on its
    World Wide Website
revamped site will allow visitors
use the site to find their way
    through the maze of
website dedicated to the Virgin
    Mary
launches a site on the web
focussing on simple themes on
    its World Wide Website
website will link to thousands of
    events
the site will remain to be ex-
    panded
the number of times a site is
    visited
download an electronic entry
    form from the website
operates a closed website
launched its Internet site
website offers access to
website has been open only a
    month
website where children will be
    able to congregate, chat and
    exchange information
website includes an interactive
    element
visit the Anglican website
on a world wide website
taken a website
started its own website

Commentary

A website is a space, but not a place, which is visited to find information, sometimes for free, or have it withdrawn (information as commodity); sites can have 'links' (part of a chain), and some of these links can bring you closer to people; information can be put 'up' on a website, and it can be 'downloaded' (information high up on a shelf); it can be 'stored' and 'loaded' (information as commodity and as ammunition); links can be 'live' (information as ammunition/electricity); a site can be 'built' on (site as building site) but it can also be 'launched' (boat/spacecraft) and is occasionally 'published' (site as publication); it can be 'owned' and sites can be 'open', 'closed' or 'licensed' to suit the operator (site as private property); sites can be dedicated to religious purposes (site as shrine).

Extension

1   The virtual environment reflects the interiors of modern corporate offices using such terms as: desktop, file, folder, filing cabinet, etc. Devise an iconic system as a means of renaming it. Files and folders used to be described using imagery of roots, trees and branches. Could you expand on that? For example, using the image of a forest or of different sized boxes. Design the icons and labels you would use. If you are really computer-proficient you might be able to build it.

2   Investigate the imagery and values of a software help file looking out for examples of informal address, marketisation and representation of business world values.

3   Compare and contrast the simulation of social space in a variety of computer programs including the words and ways that are used to encounter the user as (s)he enters and leaves the programs.

4   Subcultural languages often use language metaphorically. Gather some data together from the jargon file, *New Hacker's Dictionary* or another source. Analyse it for patterns of semantic field and use of metaphor.

5   Read Tim Rohrer's *Conceptual Blending on the Information Highway: How Metaphorical Inferences Work* at http://metaphor.uoregon.edu/iclacnf4.htm which develops the ideas outlined in this chapter with special reference to Al Gore's use of the term information superhighway.

Mailing IT – is there a language of e-mail?

Aims of this unit

This unit looks at the language of e-mail and electronic bulletin boards to see if they amount to a new variety of language. It contrasts the popular claims made about these new forms with stylistic analysis of examples and outlines some of the different approaches that have been used in research including large-scale quantitative accounts.

Activity

Carry out a small-scale survey to get an impression of the popular attitudes to e-mail. You could use the survey on the netting-it.com web-site. Questions there include the respondents' experience of e-mail and features of the e-mails they have seen or received that make the language different to speaking or writing. Alternatively, carry out a computer **keyword search** of e-mail on a newspaper CD-ROM or the Internet and note the comments made about e-mail language.

Commentary

Comments might include the idea that e-mail is less formal than writing and that correct spelling is no longer important; that it is faster than writing but allows you to read it at leisure; that it's more of a dialogue than a letter but it leaves a record – unlike a conversation; that much of it is unnecessary mass communication, particularly 'spam' advertisements and e-mails in work places; that it offers a new and exciting way of communicating.

Popular attitudes to e-mail are reflected in newspaper accounts too. The following article from a broadsheet newspaper stresses the enormity of this new communication option:

> E-mail . . . is far more than just a minor technological development for the computer literate. Its impact compares with the arrival of the Victorian railway. More than simply an accelerated horse-and-cart for the masses, trains radically altered space and time, shrinking distances and synchronising clocks across the country for the first time. So E-mail has begun to affect the way we communicate in innumerable ways.[1]

The journalist goes on to quote a range of people about their attitudes to the e-mail revolution including Terry Waite who used the opportunity of a launch of the new *Collins Dictionary* to complain about the e-mail effect on English: 'This e-mail English, bashed out without capitals, paragraphs and any idea of composition, is . . . irritating, tiring to read, and often simply unreadable'. The literary academic Frank Kermode, editor of the *Oxford Book of Letters*, finds it hard to 'imagine anyone writing a serious letter by e-mail' and comments on the way its ease of use 'fosters promiscuous communication', although he admits that there may be an *Oxford Book of Emails* one day.

Research comments

For others the more relaxed tenor of e-mail may be bound up with broader social changes towards informalisation. In their summary of e-mail research Moran and Hawisher[2] comment on the writers' attempts to personalise their texts. Other theorists have noticed the way in which e-mail can free up communication from the disciplines of literacy such as the strict conventions for letter writing. Writing some ten years before the popular use of e-mail, John Fiske contrasted the rule-bound conventions of writing with the relative freedom and functional, communicative focus of speech.[3]

It is also possible that e-mail is changing to reflect the broader and more diverse constituency of people who now use it. (In keeping with Angus Kennedy's comments on net language.)[4] In the earlier days of minority use, when e-mail was the preserve of computer enthusiasts and university academics, the vocabulary was more esoteric and exclusive and influenced by the hacker subculture. As more people start to e-mail the use of emoticons such as 'smileys' or expressions such as 'snail mail' for letter and envelope post may seem quaint to this new group.

Popular attitudes seem to suggest the novelty and freedom of e-mail relate it to a hybrid of speech and writing, but to what extent is this borne out by stylistic analysis of e-mail texts?

Activity

Read through the following e-mail text and note any features which seem to belong to speech and features that you associate with writing.

Text: E-mail between friends

Subject: Kaitlyn?

Hey Man,

How's the babe? Is that the Yankee spelling or wot?

Saw the great Moo 2 of 2 last nite but too many martinis did for me plus IMOM (creepy Jim) was in tow, bummer.

By the way I've put up my own site. I'm quite proud of myself for mastering HTML n'at (being such an old bloke). It's still in progress but you'll get the idea. Next stop, photoshop.

It can be found @ http://www.xxxxxxxxxxxxxxxxxxxx

Hope you like it (you get a link!)

Love to you and famillee

Old Lag xxxxxxx

Commentary

The text was written by M to F following the birth of her child. Underlying its informal conversation-like impressions, it is full of ironic references, which may well be more crafted than those in spontaneous unplanned conversation. It seems less formally constrained than a letter and that informality shows from the start in the address (Hey man) and then the play on 'babe': the babe of the babe and babe as a term of endearment. Both 'babe' and 'Hey man' seem to be rock archaisms – modish fashionable words from another time which now seem sexist. That intertextual reference is compounded by the way the writer describes himself as an 'old bloke' and signs himself off as 'Old Lag'. These ironic subtleties would be more likely to be picked up by a reader than a hearer.

Similarly, the written form allows verbal jokes only possible if you can see the text, such as the non-standard spellings. The slightly eccentric spelling may be a marker of an informal relaxed social relationship but it is far from haphazard. The letter is actually spelt and punctuated following the standard conventions, except for 'Yankee', 'wont,' 'nite', 'n'at' and 'famillee'. In all cases there seems to be an attitude or semantic nuance being signalled, rather like the way people put spoken words in speech marks. 'Yankee' and 'wot' play upon the spelling of the baby's name and contrast an American phonetic spelling with the British kind associated with comics like *The Beano*. 'Moo 2 of 2' and 'IMOM' are private, insider references to nicknames for friends, with the latter possibly a mock acronym. 'Nite' is now a standard non-standard spelling with possible connotations of tacky American advertising. 'N'at' softens the force of the heavy handed initialism HTML, and is actually a private allusion to an unstylish shopname with 'n'at' in it. 'Famillee' could be being flagged so it is ironic.

There are features you might associate with conversation too, including contracted forms and elliptical forms ('I've; (what a) bummer'). The latter acts like an under the breath interjection of the sort someone might make in a conversation. All but two of the paragraphs are within a single line suggesting the short turns of conversation and there are also short questions inviting replies. 'Next stop, photoshop'. This has a playful reduplication of sounds, but also is only implicitly linked to the previous sentences. It is for this reader to infer the humorous image of the old lag desperately seeking to learn new IT-related tricks.

Activity

This e-mail is from a work-related context between computer technicians and a software support engineer who are trying to identify a technical problem. Read through it and note some of the similarities and differences with the previous text.

Text: E-mail between techie colleagues

Subject: DS Dump File
From: K
To: L

Dear L

Please find attached the requested zipped files from our servers.

With regard to the creation of files for the DS Dump File, please note the following: -

1)   BALIN would not load CONFIG.NLM, so I was unable to create a Config.txt file for BALIN.

2)   I had probelms getting a DSREPAIR LOG for OIN using your guidelines, I got the following error:

"This server's DIB does not contain any replicas. This is a normal ocurance when replica distribution of partions in a directory services tree does not place any replicas on a server.   Note that you should have at least 2 replicas of every partition for fault tolerance. To perfom replica operations, run DSREPAIR on a server with replicas. Program execution should continue normally."

Well, L, it's a tall order as to what's wrong. I do appreciate all the time and effort that you have put in, you have been very helpful, I just hope that we can remedy the problem soon.

Thanks and regards,

K   :o)

Subject: Re: call 684. Update of our servers diagnostic information
From: K
To: P

Yep I have copied over CLIB.NLM from another server (and if I click right on the file in Windows Explorer and go to Properties, the file info is Modified: 2 October 1998 - the same version as the most of the other CLIB.NLMs on our other servers.

I've tried to copy one by one the 'libupi.exe' extracted files, and re-boot the server, but that hasn't worked either (oddly enough though, the server stills works OK, it's possible to still access the Information CD's on the server).

An intriguing dilemma I'm sure you'd agree, and I believe that it has someting to do with the installation of the SP6.0a patch.

Kind Regards,

K   :o(

P wrote:

> *Have you tried copying from another server and then rebooting the server?*

> >>> **From: K**
> Hi P
>
> Thanks for your email: -
>
> I've typed MODULES CLIB on our server console for BALIN, and unfortunately nothing comes up, however, when I type MODULES CLIB
> for the other servers I get the following results: -
>
> Server OIN = Ver. 4.11o   Date= 2nd October 1998
> Server KILI = Ver. 4.11O   Date= 2nd October 1998
>
> **   Server BILBO = Ver. 4.11o   Date= 7th October 1998
>
> I am wondering whether an error occured in the 6.0a patch installation for BALIN, which is causing it to go haywire with CLIB .
>
> Kind Regards,
>
> K

Commentary

This is part of an exchange between three technologically informed computer technicians discussing software problems and there is an obvious difference in the use of elaborate field-specific language to the extent that computer labels and processes become embedded in the text: 'I have copied over CLIB.NLM'; 'I've typed MODULES CLIB'.

The language here mixes human and computer language, with some conventions to stop confusion including capitals for file names and quotes for the syntax computer displays. The technical language includes acronyms and words used in a specialist manner for their metaphoric properties ('zipped'; 'patch' — a kind of repair on a program). There appears to be considerable shared technical expertise along with the need to communicate with precision and explicitness. There are few **deictic** constructions and the sequence of e-mails is spelled and punctuated with conventional standard regularity bar five minor errors.

These examples contain details of both formal letter writing and informal speech: the first letter begins and ends like a conventional letter and all the letters from K end 'Kind regards'. Two letters also include simple emoticons. One letter begins 'Yep' like a casual spoken reply.

Speech, writing and mixed modes

One common idea about e-mail is that it mixes features of speech and writing. David Crystal[5] has identified major points of contrast between speech and writing caused by the different constraints of each mode and the cultural expectations that have grown up around them. These are summarised in Table 9.1.

Table 9.1 Modes of speech and writing (after Crystal 1997)

Speech	Writing
Speech happens in real time with participants usually present.	Writing is spacebound, static and permanent.
Spontaneity and speed make it hard to plan talk, leading to looser expression and re-phrasing.	It allows careful re-reading and tends to promote more compact expression and complex grammar.
Clues such as facial expression and gesture can aid meaning and allow vague expressions such as those and that (deictics).	Lack of visual contact means that participants cannot rely on context to make their meanings clear.
Prosodic features such as intonation, loudness, tempo, rhythm, pronunciation and tone are part of the effect of speech and can be only approximated by writing.	Some more difficult grammatical constructions are more likely in writing.
Certain types of informal language such as obscenity and slang are more likely in speech.	Writing can act as a record to be revisited and re-read at leisure.
Speech is suited to social or phatic conversations where opinions and nuances can be expressed by prosody and extra-linguistic features.	Writing can be re-drafted later.
Once something is said it cannot be unsaid or altered – speech is an event.	Writing includes many spatial features, some of which cannot be spoken (tables, graphs), but has limited prosodic features.

Look through the e-mails in this book and on the website netting-it.com and list their features and possibilities in comparison to Crystal's observations as summarised in Table 9.1.

E-mails do not happen in real time and they are spacebound, although not necessarily static or permanent like ink on paper. They are between participants but the identities of those participants may not be real and the relationship may exist entirely in the correspondence. They are not spontaneous like conversation but the technology facilitates instant replies more quickly than many forms of writing – encouraging a type of time-delayed written dialogue. Clues about intonation and loudness cannot be conveyed orally, although some e-mailers use graphical means of showing pseudo-prosodic features, such as capitals for shouting and emotional stances – smileys, flames and emoticons. The reply function on e-mail does allow participants to check each other's meanings so there is not the same need for the message to be fully composed and explicit. E-mail acts as a record which can be re-read for reference, but it tends not to be composed formally as a final draft and final publication. Its status may be more provisional, as in a conversation. As an electronic text e-mail can be redrafted and re-presented seamlessly. Content can have permanence but not necessarily fixity. There will be an electronic record of the e-mail having been sent and a sequence of e-mails may leave a trail of addresses.

The conventional concerns for accurate, formal, Standard English appear to be more relaxed. E-mails can be sent automatically and directly to other participants, including being forwarded or copied by the recipient without the sender knowing. Intimate text can become very public. This can even happen accidentally when the wrong button is hit.[6]

Looking at this list we can see a combination of speech and writing features and then features not found in either (the ability to be able to copy instantly). Some of these features exist because of the physical constraints of the mode such as the screen text. Others are there because of the nature of the discussion and its participants – they are use/user related rather than mode related.

Research on e-mail and asynchronous CMC

A particular academic focus has been the comparison of electronic text with varieties of speech and writing to compare the statistical frequency of language features with norms from those modes. Some of this has taken a corpus-based approach in which large volumes of computer-mediated communication (CMC) text are searched for patterns in the frequency and variety of 'text strings' associated with types of social purpose: so the use of 'that' clauses may indicate the degree of informational elaboration. Using a model developed by Douglas Biber (1988), patterns in the co-occurrence of types of text string may indicate 'textual dimensions' such as those between informational versus involved writing, non-narrative versus narrative, situation-dependent versus explicit, overt expression of persuasion, non-abstract versus abstract information and degrees of informational elaboration. In the words of Collot and Belmore:

> Biber's particular innovation has been the analysis of computer readable corpora to determine sets of linguistic features whose presence or absence correlates with what he calls 'textual dimensions'. A textual dimension is a functional categorisation, which cuts across traditional genre classifications. The assumption is that if a particular set of linguistic features consistently co-occurs in a group of texts, that set of features serves a particular communicative function.[7]

The corpus approach has been adapted for different focuses but in general it has tended to confirm that CMC language reflects social patterns found in research based on speech and writing data, and shows a slightly different profile of language feature frequencies to those found in speech and writing. For example, both Herring and Petrie[8] make findings about differences in male and female language behaviour that are in keeping with other gender research. Herring started with the hypothesis that men were more likely to use bulletin board postings for information and women to maintain social relationships. Investigation of data did not support this but Herring did discover statistical frequencies in the stances taken towards the previous messages. Male approaches were often more adversarial and oppositional whereas women were more likely to develop their postings from previous messages.

From a formal stance of mode comparisons, Collot and Belmore researched bulletin board postings to find patterns of text string frequency that placed CMC between speech and writing. Yates researched variety of vocabulary use with a type/token method where every word in a hundred being different scored 100 and every word being the same scores 1.[9] He found the lexical variety of computer mediated communication closer to writing than speech although there was a greater use of first- and second-person pronouns than in either speech or writing, possibly highlighting the interpersonal focus of the variety.

The most significant recent UK research on this topic was a survey based upon over 38,000 British e-mails by Professor Helen Petrie. Her provisional results show some unsurprising gendered differences in use of e-mail including women using it more to communicate about relationships and personal states and feelings in contrast to more information and content-focused male text. She makes a number of interesting observations about different types of e-mailer profile, outlining some generational trends underlying this new type of communication and coins the word 'emailism' for stylistic features which are rare in handwriting and/or typed communications but which occur commonly in e-mails. Some 55.37 per cent of e-mails sent by her participants contain at least one although her general impression is that participants are using 'fairly standard written English in all its aspects – spelling, punctuation, grammar and style'. She notes that the four most frequent e-mailisms are 'ways of trying to convey emotion in written email form with very simple manipulations of the standard character set. Whereas the use of "smilies" or emoticons was very rare'; see Figure 9.1.

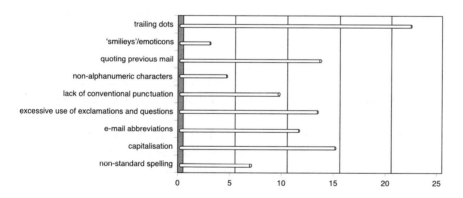

Figure 9.1 Frequency of 'emailisms' (after Petrie 1999)

Petrie's approach is from a psychologist's standpoint and language students might want to examine the rationale behind some aspects of the research including the idea of 'excessive' use of exclamations and questions, and the grouping of keyboard shortcut acronyms with 'unconventional punctuation'. Spelling errors that might be a mistake were ignored.

89

Summary

This unit has compared some popular beliefs about e-mail with academic findings that suggest that the language is less dramatically different than is sometimes suggested. You should be aware of some of the approaches that can be used to investigate this new variety, from stylistic analysis to large-scale quantitative approaches.

Extension

The research above is based upon postgraduate linguistic expertise and access to specialist corpora and equipment but you can still sample the approach in small-scale qualitative studies based on your own data. You may even have the opportunity to look at varieties about which there is little research. You may find it useful to look up and read some Internet sites with accounts of e-mail research. Start by accessing Petrie's findings on http://147.197.156.153/NetResearch/Reports/Email%20Study/InitialReport.htm

1   Investigating patterns of e-mail as a variety. Try building a small-scale corpus of e-mails by using the edit, cut and paste commands to transfer the e-mails to a separate document. This is to get rid of the machine text at the top, which would confuse the spellchecker. Then run through the text with a spellchecker to see how many words are spelt using non-standard forms (this won't pick up **homophones** such as 'there' and 'they're') but you could discount these as you work through the spellchecker. Then try doing the same using some word-processed letters.

2   Are Petrie's findings about e-mail true of the language used by you and your peers? Carry out an investigation combining stylistic analysis, small corpus analysis and interviews. Present your findings using tables and graphs.

3   What different genres can you find in e-mail and what are their main features? Here are some suggestions: varieties of chain e-mail including hoax warnings, sales letters, charity appeals, student to student letters and e-jokes and puzzles.

4   Bulletin board discussions can be very specialised according to the topic focus of the group. Record and analyse a particular type of discussion. For example, an initial look at the discussion groups hosted by computer magazines showed marked informality, teasing and taboo-breaking humour along with technical field-specific

reference. The choice of identifying names was an object of study in its own right.

5   At the time of writing (January 2000) there is some evidence that the word for electronic post is stabilising around the spelling 'email' in preference to hyphenated form (e-mail), the version with capitalised E (E-mail) and the unshortened compound word (electronic mail). UK texts from the early 1990s used the word electronic post before the US influence substituted mail for post. In the late 1990s the E shortening of electronic is forming a vogue affix in such constructions as E-commerce. Use the methods in Unit 7 to investigate the history of the word including identifying critical changes from forms in inverted commas, unhyphenated compounds, and the shortening of 'electronic' to 'e'.

Speaking IT in writing – chat language and identity

Aims of this unit

This unit looks at the more obvious stylistic features of electronic 'chat-rooms' where participants use writing and symbols to 'chat' in real time. The unit begins by describing the features and properties of chat and the issues arising from it, and then outlines some of the varied research approaches. This is no more than an introduction to the most complex and bizarre of the new communication technology text types and the aim of the unit is to map some investigation pathways for the reader to take further.

What is IWD?

In 'interactive written discourse' (IWD) participants word process conversational turns in an online written simulated conversation.[1] Such discourse can take many forms including casual open-ended 'chat' and complex specialist role playing games such as those in multi-user dungeons (MUDs). The different genres are described in some of the books and on the website.[2]

Unlike e-mail which is **asynchronous**: IWD communication occurs in real time with minimal delay between turns. This and the requirement for typing give it an unusual dynamic tension between the need to respond quickly in real time but having to use a keyboard to do it. Another strange factor is the lack of contextual anchorage that might be provided by IRL physical cues of appearance, body language or physical manifestation of text. The conversation involves participants who arrive in a virtual space or 'room' with an identity which is usually not their real name and which may disguise age, gender and other aspects of IRL identity. Simulating a different identity or outlook is common practice and there is even the hacker sense of the word '**trolling**' for deliberately misleading identity and behaviour designed to provoke a response.[3]

The various types of chat including IRC, MUDs, MOOs have existed for many years although used only by small numbers of expert specialists. For example, MUDs began in the late 1970s as a means of playing role playing adventure games using computers.[4] The ease of use of the Internet is making text-based chat much more accessible as no special protocols have to be learned. This and the rapid expansion in ownership of networked computers have encouraged growth of such chat forums as those provided by **Geocities**[5] and the constituency of users is much wider and more numerous than used to be the case. This may have reduced the level of commitment and co-operative behaviour displayed in some rooms. Some other older specialist types of chat such as MOOs require programming skills and remain more of a specialist subculture although nearly all types of IWD have some participants, the operators (sysops), with superior powers coming from technical knowledge and not available to others.

Activity

Read through the following text and list some of the features you associate with speech, with writing and with electronic text. Look again at the features of speech, writing and e-mail in Table 9.1. What situational constraints and opportunities are there in IWD that set it apart from these other modes?

Text: Chat room

Talk about anything you like. (Obnoxiousness tolerated but not encouraged.)

There are 3 people here

Kokie : no Oklahoma is not all that green we are from Ohio but live here now..the part of oklahoma we are in is called GreenCountry..but not like ohio..this is cattle countryt...yeahaa..cowboys...
[April 18, 1998 14:15:06]

wrecker : LadyJ, can I leave you with Kokie, I really need to hang up the phone now ? byeee.
[April 18, 1998 14:15:50]

Kokie : whatis your problem with icq I may be able to help
[April 18, 1998 14:15:59]

Dream Maker® : You here yet.....
[April 18, 1998 14:16:07]

Ladyj : When I first came to the USA we lived in Mansfield Ohio..I liked it there..
[April 18, 1998 14:16:33]

Kokie : Oh no Ladyj I lived in Bucyrus for years and my sister in law is in Mansfield...small world...
[April 18, 1998 14:18:11]

Kokie : Ladyj is having problems with ICQ Dream
[April 18, 1998 14:19:27]

Ladyj : I used to pronounce Bucyrus Buck-e-rus..I was laughed at..
[April 18, 1998 14:20:03]

Kokie : was the Bratwurst Festival going on when you were there at bucyrus..we were there last year ..
[April 18, 1998 14:20:58]

Ladyj : I loved Kingwood Center in the spring..is that the right name..
[April 18, 1998 14:21:33]

Kokie : wonder how many Jane Smiths there are..a bunch..maybe Jane x Smith will do
[April 18, 1998 14:21:59]

Ladyj : No don't remember that one..We spent alot of time canoeing the mohican..
[April 18, 1998 14:23:14]

Kokie : I miss Ohio but not the winters..I would like to live there in the summer..we were born and raised in Lima..
[April 18, 1998 14:23:17]

Commentary

Conversational features include interactivity and numbers of partici-pants, the written elements include its visual form. The new technology properties would also include it being searchable, saveable ASCII text. In e-mail, text has to be word processed and it was argued that this could be done casually without worrying about perfect spelling. In IWD there is the constraint of having to compose messages very quickly in order for them to be 'heard' in time for them to make sense in context. This practical consideration may well override accuracy of spelling.

In e-mail, messages are often dyadic (between two people). Even where text can be sent to multiple audiences it is on a one-to-one basis. In IWD there may be a number of participants present and a number of conversational strands.

In e-mail the writer has control of the topic in the sense they cannot be interrupted half-way through the message and there is no need or no opportunity for the audience to respond with minimal responses. Like a letter, the message can be as long as it needs to be. In IWD a long turn 'hogs the conversation' keeping other participants out.

In a chat room there may be many participants interacting and several threads of conversation co-existing. People can't quite talk at once because only one textline at a time appears on the screen, nor can they focus on a conversation with one other participant unless they break off from the group and go into another room. Dialogue may be stranded with several threads and a reply may refer to a comment several messages back. 'Disparate strands of conversation are juxtaposed forming sequences that intertwine to form a multi-dimensional text'.[6]

In IWD participants are more likely to feel the need for reassurance from other participants and there are conventions around greeting others as they arrive and go, and responding to jokes with laughter. The real-time contexts and the lack of contextual clues create a situational need for the kinds of interpersonal behaviour which in speech is provided by the paralinguistic clues of pitch, volume, intonation and body language. Along with text there is the convention of using symbols, either pictures or 'alphabetical rebuses' (symbols made with letters) to provide these clues.

In e-mail the writer can choose whom to communicate with and in many cases it will be someone they know over a period of time and in a variety of situational contexts. In IWD people can 'pair off' in a new room but there may be less choice of influence over the participants and much less knowledge about them. They are as they are presented and that presentation may not relate to the IRL self.[7]

95

In e-mail, conversation appears private. Many forms of chat are refereed by a participant/operator with access to technology that can exclude people from the group, eject them or silence them. Other participants may also have access to the technological version of sticking their fingers in their ears by placing them in a 'kill file'.

The formal features of IWD

In one of the earlier stylistic studies of chat Christopher Werry sees the new language features of IWD as an attempt to simulate speech: 'an almost manic tendency to produce auditory and visual effects in writing, a straining to make written words imitate speech'.[8] The new language has similar opportunities to those provided by contextual clues (supra-segmentals, paralanguage and actions) in spoken language and gives the scrolling text a greater sense of emphasis and identity than the plain font would otherwise allow. According to Werry, the limitations of screen size, typing speed, and response times lead to features of brevity and abbre-viation to reduce the demands of the keyboard, paralinguistic clues to 'create the effects of spoken delivery' and actions and gestures to simulate the kind of social gestures which might take place in the physical contexts of real-life conversations. The following summarises some of his main observations.

A tendency towards brevity and minimal number of keyboard strokes including

- short turns averaging six words;
- heavily abbreviated forms with letters left out (Tu es + T'es in French);
- words left out (deletion of I pronoun);
- letter homophones (Are you = RU);
- 'key bindings ' of letter homophones standing for phrases (Cyal8r, IMHO).

Paralinguistic prosodic clues give a sense of the effects of spoken delivery:

- reduplicated letters for emphasis (sooo slooow) – sometimes used to disrupt as in 'flooding';
- periods and hyphens to break up conversation (And . . .);
- capitalisation for emphasis;
- colloquial and phonetic spelling (fx = effects).

Actions and gestures are also used:

- ◎ 'alphabetical rebuses', or letter pictures (@}-`-,`-,` -= rose);
- ◎ rituals and gifts (Champagne all round).

Since Werry wrote this and as technology has developed, these alphabetical rebuses are being replaced by graphics symbols taken from emoticon 'banks' provided by the chatroom provider.

Werry also comments on the ironic playfulness of IWD and the tendency for participants to mix and match language to create a 'bricolage of discursive fragments drawn from songs, TV characters and a variety of different social speech types'. This is related to the new text type being free from the conventions and expectations (the 'determinate contexts') of previous forms such as letters, and disinhibited by the anonymity of the participants.

Activity

Werry wrote his study in the mid-1990s when chat was still a specialist subculture. How true are his ideas now? Collect some examples of Internet chat from the website and consider them in relation to Werry's description.

Virtual identity

A number of researchers have commented on the psycho-social dimensions of CMC and especially the effects of a lack of the social cues provided by face-to-face presence. These are reported extensively in Herring (1996), usefully summarised by Moran and Hawisher in Snyder (1997) and Kollock and Smith (1999) and Jones (1998). For example, Ma's[9] study of transnational bulletin board conferencing led him to comment on the tendency of participants to share personal information but without commitment or interest in the consequences of that sharing. Other earlier studies explained aggressive online behaviour as coming from the lack of embarrassing constraints that would occur in face-to-face conversation. It was also thought that the lack of such constraints might allow exploration of gender identities. More recently research comment has focused on the concept of disinhibition. The lack of contextual clues frees up social inhibition but also loosens commitment and trust in the group. Free from such inhibitions behaviours may ape and exaggerate the stereotyping within a culture as in the hyper-gendered behaviour of male participants representing themselves as women of male stereotyped variety. In 'Managing the virtual commons',[10] Kollock and Smith examine the co-operative principles underlying the way in which the **virtual community** organises itself, looking at the co-operative behaviours which encourage people to give back to the shared electronic environment (the virtual commons) as well as take, and the negotiation of codes of conduct which regulate behaviour.

Extension

This unit is introductory and you are advised to research more widely before investigating further in chatrooms. The website by John Suler would make a starting point: http://www.rider.edu/users/suler/psycyber/psycyber.html

IWD includes the strangest and most distinctive new genres of computer-mediated communication and they are the least researched. The sexual overtones of some chat makes it advisable to be cautious, particularly in the disclosure of personal details and e-mail addresses. Familiarise yourself with netiquette conventions and observe before seeking to join in.

1   Record and make transcriptions of three spontaneous casual conversations and an equivalent amount of IWD chat. Use this as the basis for a close comparison using language study concepts from discourse and conversation analysis. Develop your enquiry by making comparisons between the number of participants and contextual similarities and differences, length of turns, topic boundary marking and greetings. As you become more familiar with the data you may want to develop a more specific focus such as **phatic communion** or topic development.

2   A useful investigation could be made by looking at the names people choose to represent themselves. Other aspects to consider would be the questions used to establish the identities of interlocutors including patterns in the focus on age and gender. Judith Donath's essay[11] will give you fascinating and hilarious background ideas for this. See also Brenda Danet's CMC net journal, volume 1, issue 2 on http://www.ascusc.orgljcmc

3   From the beginning of CMC in MUDs participants have been focused on the collaborative writing of simulated IRL experiences from rooms to sexual encounters and the pleasures of participating in the 'consensual hallucination' has been commented on by many. Investigate some of the means by which chat rooms or MUDs simulate the

sense of a parallel world including looking at the interpersonal language that makes the social space and gestures and simulated physical realities of the parallel IRL world. For a reference on MUDs see the specialist site: mud.co.uk/richard and especially 'MUD-writings Archive'.

4   Gather together some data from chatrooms and analyse these for linguistic means by which participants establish power, co-operation and competition. Compare these findings with ideas taken from the analysis of transcripts of spoken language. Students working on this have suggested that simulated US accent features have higher prestige and have noted cruising obstructive behaviour characterised by 'flooding' text with repeated keyboard strokes.

5   Look up and print out some versions of 'netiquette' statements. Compare and contrast these with H.P. Grice's (1967) ideas about **conversational maxims** and implicatures.

Researching IT – using ICT to investigate language

- ◎ *Guidance*: There is accessible guidance on researching and writing up language investigation projects in: M. Sebba (1995*) Focussing on Language: A student's guide to researching and writing up language projects*, Lancaster: Definite Article Publications and A. Wray, K. Trott, A. Bloomer with S. Reay and C. Butler (1998) *Projects in Linguistics: A practical guide to researching language*, London: Arnold. The latter includes introductions to statistics and corpus-based study and a section on the data protection implications of computer records.

- ◎ *Research ethics and confidentiality*: ICT creates a growing virtual archive of recorded electronic text of all varieties;[1] using it is more than a matter of cut, edit and paste. There are ethical and legal responsibilities including those protecting confidentiality and copyright. Permission should be sought for electronic text and particularly e-mails and private correspondence. As with transcripts, such material needs to be treated to remove the references to names, places and other identifying features.[2]

- ◎ *Researching and searching with IT-computer-assisted methods*: Computer-assisted language investigation can be attempted with a word processor, CD-ROM reference and standard spreadsheet software, as demonstrated in Unit 7. More developed approaches need a specialist program such as Wordsmith Tools. The BNC Sampler version of the British National Corpus contains a 2 million

101

word 2 per cent sample of the BNC and four software text analysis packages customised to work with the BNC (including Wordsmith Tools). This provides a practical introduction to the methods of computer-assisted language analysis although the sample corpus is not large enough for reliable results.

◎ *Copying and pasting text*: Make up an electronic data scrapbook by copying and pasting text into a word-processor file. Save it in ASCII or RTF format. The availability of cheaper scanners with OCR makes it possible to convert and save typed text.

◎ *Spellchecker and grammar checkers*: Spellcheckers and grammar checkers represent a version of the standard language and can be used to make a first check about whether a word/phrase is seen as accepted usage. These programs, or tools as they like to be known, often represent a conservative, business-oriented version of Standard English, sometimes of an American variety.

◎ *Text searches*: Electronic text searches for key words or text strings can be a quick and productive way of gathering data . You could also try more advanced searches such as the use of **wildcards** or **Boolean searches** where a word is searched for in proximity to other specified words. Such data can be copied and pasted into a home-made KWIC list. It can be used to develop the kind of simple statistical work suggested in Unit 8.

◎ *Word frequency profiles*: Some programs will process text to produce statistical accounts of word frequency. **Function words** are usually most frequent but patterns in the **lexical words** will be more revealing and can indicate thematic concerns. The semantic fields or lexical cohesion can be compared with those for other texts or other benchmarks.

◎ *Concordancing and KWIC lists*: Programs will also identify collocates or co-occurring words and display these in KWIC lists. This makes it possible to see patterns in how a word is used in its contexts.

◎ *Type/token counts*: A method for assessing breadth of vocabulary in use: a text repeating the same word 100 times would score 1/100 and a text using 100 different words 100/100.[3]

◎ *Tagged files and parsing*: Tagged files in some language corpora enable more complex grammar-related searches.

◎ *Writing up investigations in outlining or HTML*: Hierarchical text organisation in outlining tools and HTML allows new ways of presenting findings. There are some examples of this in the online *JCMC* (see http://www.ascusc.org/jcmc/: see volume 1, issue 2, edited by Brenda Danet).

index of terms

acronym 38

A word formed by taking the first letters of a compound word or phrase in which the consonant/vowel sequence allows the whole to be pronounced as a word and not as a sequence of letters. Examples: radar and NATO – not BBC (which is an initialism).

asynchronous 92

Communication which occurs with delays between turns (e.g. email). Synchronous: communication with turns taken in real time (e.g. Internet chat, video conferencing).

anorak 39

Derogatory term used about computer enthusiasts or de-socialised enthusiasts generally; (see also **geek** and **nerd**). Geek and nerd have more a specific sense of computer enthusiast whereas anorak seems to comment on poor social skills. There is an Internet genre of spoof nerd questionnaires and fashion advice sites. All these words have negative connotations as against the more positive expert or radical roles suggested by 'techie' or 'hacker'. A subject for further language investigation.

baud 35

An information flow measurement of one byte per second.

bleaching 56

A situation in which a word loses some of its original force and specificity. 'Bloody' no longer carries the force it did when it was a blasphemous phrase ('By Our Lady') in a predominantly Catholic Christian culture.

blend 54

A word formed by two or three free morphemes combined and shortened to form a new word which incorporates the meanings of the constituents (e.g. Internet, and 'etiquette' to 'netiquette').

Boolean search 102

A more complex type of keyword search that gives the user the choice of looking for a word with, or not with, another word.

booting, bootstrapping 38

The start-up process in which a computer reminds itself of its existence in a sequence of command controls that flash on the screen before it becomes operational. Said to come from a start-up program called bootstrap loader which was popular in the 1980s.

machine-readable signals of zeros and noughts: turning atoms into bits, to paraphrase Negroponte (1995).

emoticon 6

A **blend** of emotion and icons: symbols such as **smileys** used to express emotional attitudes and nuances. Originally keyboard-created and now often taking the form of small graphical images or thumbnails.

function words 102

Words with a grammatical rather than a lexical function such as articles, determiners, and prepositions. Such words occur more frequently in texts than content or lexical words but say less about field and domain. They could be seen as the grammatical mortar that frames and sticks together the lexical bricks.

geek 39

See **anorak**.

Geocities 93

The name of a mass-appeal website for virtual communities who come together around shared interests and not shared time or space: an IRL simulation of the city.

hacker 11

The *Oxford Dictionary of New Words* distinguishes between the colloquial meaning of a person who enjoys programming or computers for their own sake and a more specific sense of someone who uses computer expertise to gain unauthorised access to computer networks. A CD-ROM keyword search shows

the latter is becoming the predominant meaning in terms of number of hits. Hacker has undergone pejoration with increasing connotations of subversive or criminal activity.

handshake 77

A metaphorical expression to refer to the exchange of computer protocols by fax machines when they connect. Sometimes used verbally or iconically about similar Internet connection.

homophone 90

Two different words (lexemes) which sound the same or similar: there, they're and their are obvious examples.

hypernyms 57

These are overarching categories under which constituent words can be grouped.

hyponym 49

Lettuce and cabbage are co-hyponyms of the hypernym term vegetable.

icon 74

In language study, something iconic is a direct representation of something as opposed to something symbolic which suggests its referent more indirectly. Icon has also come to mean a graphical symbol that can be manipulated to control a computer program.

imperative 18

Another word for a command. In terms of formal grammatical function, sentences can command (imperative), state (declarative), ask (interrogative) or exclaim (exclamatory).

informalisation 24

A style of writing that suggests an easy-going social relationship between writer and reader, based on informal address terms, direct address to the reader with the second-person pronoun, and casual colloquial expressions. (Goodman 1996: 142.)

keyword search 80

A computer search in which the machine searches for matches of a pattern of strings of code or ASCII characters in sequence.

KWIC list 50

These are computer-generated lists of characters or words in their immediate contexts. These are generated by such programs as Wordsmith Tools and the BNC SARA interface. They can be used to search for situational uses and textstrings, including letters, words and **smileys**.

leakage 50

A type of semantic widening in which a word leaks out of its original function to other contexts. So 'joyriding' may be used loosely for its metaphorical sense of reckless pleasure-seeking.

lexical words 102

These include those in word classes such as nouns, verbs, adjectives and adverbs. These often reveal patterns of meaning or **semantic fields** in a text.

marketisation 24

The informalisation of style and the mixing of persuasion and information for marketing purposes. (Goodman 1996: 142.)

mining (data mining) 2

A word or phrase used in the business sections of some broadsheets to refer to the detailed computer-assisted examination of computer databases in order to generate commercial, political or legal intelligence. Storecards and Internet choice histories can be used in this way.

multi-modal 9

Mode refers to a channel of communication: a multi-modal text combines different channels of communication such as sight, movement and audio stimuli.

narratee 27

The reader implied by the text: the ideal reader who shares the assumptions and the values the text appears to promote.

nerd 39

See **anorak**.

netiquette 54

Politeness conventions for using e-mails.

over-lexicalisation 38

This refers to a situation in which there are considerably more words for a referent than are needed for precise communication, possibly implying that the purposes of the words are for social display, competition and performance. It could be argued that such words have a primary interpersonal function (Halliday 1978: 166).

paralinguistic 21
A means of conveying meaning outside verbal language. Non-verbal communication is paralinguistic.

phatic communion 98
The type of exchange which is redundant in terms of instrumental meaning but socially significant (Malinowski 1923).

pre-modification/pre-modifiers 29
The positioning of adjectives and other modifiers before that which they describe or modify. These often take the form of single words or lists of single words. As distinct from post-modification which occurs after the noun or verb described and often takes the form of a phrase or clause (e.g. 'The red chicken' as opposed to 'the chicken that was red').

prosodic 18
Auditory features such as stress, volume, pitch and intonation that indicate how words should be interpreted.

pseudo-prosodic features 18
Use of graphological features in CMC such as capitalisation to indicate shouting or non-standard spellings to indicate how a word should be pronounced ('kewl' for 'cool', 'seeing ya' for 'seeing you').

referent 38
That which is referred to.

re-lexicalise 38
This refers to the process in which lexical words are re-used for other referents, particularly as practised by marginalised or oppositional social groups who may create elaborate alternative vocabularies. Such words may show patterns of logic, jokes, insider knowledge or metaphorical extension (e.g. crashing cheat = teeth; smelling cheat = nose; belly cheat = apron: Halliday 1978: 173).

semantic, semantic widening 48
Related to meaning. Semantic field refers to the patterns of meaning in a text; semantic widening refers to a process in which a word develops a more generalised meaning than it had previously; semantic narrowing refers to its developing a narrowed and more specific sense.

semantic fields 72
A field of meaning. May be a narrow related gradeable field such as temperature (hot – tepid – luke warm – cold) or more loosely connected meanings of a related type such as terms associated with love or romance.

shibboleth 35
A sociolinguistic concept with an Old Testament etymology: a word, the use of which can be used as a marker of group identity. Knowing it means you are part of the group; not knowing leaves you an outsider. See Judges xii, 4–6.

smileys 6
See **emoticon**.

Electronic junk mail, or sending it.

A word used by some computer theorists to refer to deliberate extended iconic metaphors in computer interfaces. If the text saved is a document, then it will be saved in a filing cabinet or may be thrown in a wastepaper bin, by analogy with an IRL office.

A taboo is an aspect of experience which is forbidden in a particular culture. It is said that sex, death and cancer are taboos in the UK. Taboo-breaking means language or behaviour which wilfully crosses these thresholds.

The social relationship implied and enacted by a text or discourse: its underlying politics and assumptions as indicated by formality, politeness, address and clues about implied hierarchy. See Halliday (1978).

A letter or sequence of characters that can be searched and manipulated by a computer. All ASCII text can be combined in text strings that relate to computer code. Scanned images such as digitised graphics, audio or video cannot be searched directly in this way although information can be searched by ASCII-based headers such as file or track details.

Impersonating a fictitious identity online in order to enrage other users and provoke them into flaming. See Donath (1999).

This test was devised by computer theorist Alan Turing in 1950 to measure artificial intelligence. Also called the 'imitation game', the test is whether a computer could be detected in a typed dialogue between a computer and a person. A person and a machine each have a typed conversation with a questioner, who has to decide which is the human and which is the computer. If they guess wrong half the time, the computer passes Turing's Test.

Groups of people who maintain contact through computer-mediated communication such as chat rooms or MUDs as opposed to f2f contact.

A blank used in a keyword search. So joyrid— will produce results for joyride, joyrider and joyriding.

notes

Introduction

1   Ilana Synder (1998).
2   See H. Petrie's figures for 1999 e-mail use in http://147.197.156.153/NetResearch/Reports/Email%20Study/InitialReport.htm
3   See H. Petrie's classification of different types of e-mailers in http://147.197.156.153/NetResearch/Reports/Email%20Study/InitialReport.htm
4   Donna Haraway (1991).
5   Andrew Gauntlett (1999).
6   S.C. Herring (1996).

1: What is IT? - the nature of electronic text

1   Ted Nelson (1987).
2   K.M.E. Murray (1977).
3   For example, Caroline Spurgeon (1952).
4   Reported to me by Saint Brendan's IT technicians.
5   Andrew Gauntlett (1999).
6   See Eugene F. Provenzo Jr (1995) 'The Electronic Panopticon: censorship control and indoctrination in a post typographic culture', in M. Tuman.
7   Michael Herne, cited by Jay David Bolter in Myron Tuman (1992).
8   See also Diane Balestri *et al.* (1992).
9   See media accounts of the Stop the City and Seattle World Trade riots in August/December 1999.
10 Reported by Chris Shelly to author, 1999.
11 Rob Pope (1998).

2: Laying IT out - graphology and multi-modal texts

1   Sir C. Burt (1950) *A Psychological Study of Typography*, London: Cambridge University Press. Cited in S. Goodman and D. Graddol (1996). See Goodman (1996) for more detailed treatment.
2   'The single, exclusive, intensive focus on written language has dampened the full development of all kinds of human potentials in all kinds of respects, cognitively and affectively, in two- and three-

dimensional literacy.' G. Kress (1998) 'Visual and verbal modes of representation in electronically mediated communication', in I. Snyder.
3   S. Goodman (1996) 'Visual English', in S. Goodman and D. Graddol.
4   Kress, op. cit.
5   This will be apparent to anyone who has found themselves accidentally
     propelled online by their computer because they have typed an e-mail
     or web address.
6   Semantic nuance is used by David Crystal (1995).
7   Private bulletin board exchange, 1995.
8   *Financial Times,* Information Technology supplement, 1992.

3: Selling IT - how new technologies are represented

1   G. Kress (1998) 'Visual and verbal modes of represenation in electroni-
     cally mediated communication', in I. Synder.
2   Ibid.
3   Norman Fairclough (1992).
4   Geoffrey Leech, quoted by Norman Fairclough.
5   See G.C. Beaton's summary of Weizenbaum and Eliza dialogue on
     http://writers.ngapartji.com.au/writers/gcbeaton/eliza.htm
6   M. McGrath (1998), p. 197.
7   Sadie Plant (1998), p. 91.

4: Specialising in IT - jargons and subcultures

1   M.A.K. Halliday (1978).
2   Walter Nash (1993).
3   M. McGrath (1998), p. 144.
4   Ibid., p. 128.
5   Eric S. Raymond (1996).
6   Elizabeth Knowles (1997) *The Oxford Dictionary of New Words.*

5: Naming IT - how new words enter the language

1   J. Algeo (1999).
2   *Oxford English Dictionary* on CD ROM (*OED2*).
3   See S. Yates, summarised in S. Graddol and D. Goodman (1996).
4   Paul du Gay *et al.* (1997).
5   Ted Nelson (1992) 'Opening Hypertext: a memoir', in M. Tuman.
6   William Gibson (1984), p. 12. (Page number from the HarperCollins 1995
     edition.)

7   *The Oxford Dictionary of New Words* gives a different account from that suggested by Dery. It links the word to fads for trainsurfing, liftsurfing and channel surfing (Knowles 1987: 303).

6: Forming IT - how new words are structured

1   Gerry Knowles (1987).
2   David Crystal (1995).
3   Jean Aitchison (1994).
4   L. Bauer (1998).
5   J. Algeo (1999: 85).
6   *Oxford English Dictionary*.
7   Lewis Carroll (1872) *Alice Through the Looking-Glass*.
8   See Bauer (1998).
9   Mike Green *Of Slang, Jargon and Techspeak* on http://www.citysun.ac.uk/aer/computer.htm

7: Watching IT - tracking new words

1   Jean Aitchison (1994).
2   *The Times*, 20 December 1992.
3   The British National Corpus, http://info.ox.ac.uk/bnc
4   Charles Arthur 'What a tangled Web we weave', *New Scientist*, 17 December 1994, p. 144.

8: Picturing IT - mapping meanings on to electronic space

1   G. Lakoff and M. Johnson (1981).

9: Mailing IT - is there a language of e-mail?

1   Peter Stanford 'Getting the message', *Sunday Times*, 4 July 1999: http//:www.sunday-times.co.uk/news/pages/sti/99/07/04/sticulcnl02003.html
2   Charles Moran and Gail Hawisher (1998) 'The rhetorics and languages of electronic mail', in I. Snyder.
3   John Fiske (1989) 'The discipline of the literate is marked by its rules of correctness, particularly those of syntax and spelling. An oralised script has no need of correct spelling and syntax. Its markers of oralisation are

its errors, its deviations (deliberate or ignorant) from the discipline of literacy. . . . Oral language is context and function oriented rather than rule oriented.'

4   Angus Kennedy (1999).
5   David Crystal (1997).
6   John Diamond 'Cretins creep in as anarchy rules', *The Times*, 17 April 1996.
7   M. Collot and N. Belmore (1996) 'Electronic languages: a new variety of English', in S.C. Herring.
8   S.C. Herring (1996); Helen Petrie (1999) *Writing in Cyberspace: A study of the uses, style and content of e-mail*: http:/www.netinvestigations.net/
9   S. Yates (1996) 'Oral and written linguistic aspects of computer conferencing', in S.C. Herring.

10: Speaking IT in writing - chat language and identity

1   C. Werry (1996) 'Linguistic and interactional features of Internet relay chat', in S.C. Herring.
2   See the Introduction to M.A. Smith and P. Kollock (1999), and J. Suler (1999).
3   See Judith S. Donath (1999) 'Identity and deception in the virtual community', in Smith and Kollock.
4   See mud.co.uk/richard/ifan294.htm
5   See Introduction to M.A. Smith and P. Kollock (1999).
6   C. Werry in S.C. Herring (1996).
7   There are various well-documented cases of audiences developing strong involved relationships with participants who have been invented. See M.A. Smith and P. Kollock (1999) and Steven Jones (1998).
8   Werry in S.C. Herring (1996).
9   Ringo Ma (1996) 'Computer-mediated conversations as a new dimension of intercultural communication between East Asian and North American college students', in S.C. Herring.
10   Marc A. Smith and Peter Kollock (1996) 'Managing the virtual commons', in S.C. Herring.
11   See note 3 above.

Appendix

1   See Marc A. Smith in M.A. Smith and P. Kollock (1999).
2   There is helpful guidance on these aspects in Chris Butler's sections in *Projects in Linguistics* which also introduces the use of computers to investigate texts and statistical methods.
3   Janet Maybin and Neil Mercer (1996).

bibliography

See the netting-it.com website for web addresses which relate to the units and for an updated bibliography.

Aitchison, Jean (1994) *Language Joyriding*, Oxford: Clarendon Press.

Algeo, John (1999) *Cambridge History of English Language*, Cambridge: Cambridge University Press.

Aston, Guy and Burnard, Lou (1998) *The BNC Handbook: Exploring the British National Corpus with SARA*, Edinburgh: Edinburgh University Press; BNC http://info.ox.ac.uk/bnc

Balestri, Diane, Ehrmann, Stephen and Ferguson, David (eds) (1992) *Learning to Design, Designing to Learn: Using technology to transform the Curriculum*, London: Taylor & Francis.

Baron, Naomi (2000) *Alphabet to Email*, London: Routledge.

Bauer, Laurie (1998) *Vocabulary*, London: Routledge.

Biber, Douglas (1988) *Variation Across Speech and Writing*, Cambridge: Cambridge University Press.

Burt, C. (1950) *A Psychological Study of Typography*, Cambridge: Cambridge University Press.

Chandler, Daniel (2000) 'Technologial or media determinism', www.aber.ac.uk/media/Documents/tecdet/tecdet.html

Collot, M. and Belmore, N. (1996) 'Electronic language: a new variety of English', in S.C. Herring *Computer-Mediated Communication*, Amsterdam: Benjamins.

Crystal, David (1995) *The Cambridge Encyclopedia of English Language*, Cambridge: Cambridge University Press.

Crystal, David (1997) *The Cambridge Encyclopedia of English Language*, 2nd edn, Cambridge: Cambridge University Press.

Crystal, David (1998) 'Interpreting interlanguage', *E*, September (http://www:e-mag.com)

Dery, Mark (1997) *Escape Velocity: Cyberculture at the end of the century*, London: Grove Press.

Diamond, John (1996) 'Cretins creep in as anarchy rules', *The Times*, 17 April.

Donath, Judith S. (1999) 'Identity and deception in the virtual community', in M.A. Smith and Peter Kollock (eds) *Communities in Cyberspace*, London: Routledge.

du Gay, Paul, Hall, Stuart and Janes, Linda *et al.* (1997) *Doing Cultural Studies: The story of the Sony Walkman*, London: Sage Publications.

Fairclough, Norman (1992) *Discourse and Social Change*, Cambridge: Polity Press.

Fiske, John (1989) *The Language of Popular Culture*, London: Routledge

Gauntlett, Andrew (1999) *Net Spies: Who's watching you on the web?*, London: Vision.

Gibson, William (1984) *Neuromancer*, London: Gollancz.

Goodman, Sharon (1996) 'Visual English', in S. Goodman and D. Graddol (eds) *Redesigning English*, London: Routledge.

Goodman, Sharon and Graddol, David (eds) (1996) *Redesigning English: New texts, new identities*, London: Routledge.

Grice, H.P. (1967) 'Logic and conversation', in P. Cole and J.L. Morgan (eds) *Syntax and Semantics*, Vol. 3, New York: Academic Press.

Halliday, M.A.K. (1978) *Language as Social Semiotic*, London: Arnold.

Haraway, Donna A. (1991) *Simians, Cyborgs and Women: The re-invention of nature*, London: Free Association Books.

Herring, S.C. (ed.) (1996) *Computer-Mediated Communication: Linguistic, social and cross-cultural perspectives*, Amsterdam: Benjamins.

Jones, Steven G. (1998) *CyberSociety 2.0: Re-visiting computer-mediated communication*, London: Sage Publications.

Journal of Computer-Mediated Communication (http://www.ascusc.org/jcmc/) see volume 1, issue 2, edited by Brenda Danet.

Kennedy, Angus J. (1999) *Rough Guide to the Internet*, London: Rough Guides.

Knowles, Elizabeth with Julia Elliott (1997) *The Oxford Dictionary of New Words*, Oxford: Oxford University Press.

Knowles, G.R. (1987) *Patterns of Spoken English*, London: Longman.

Kress, G.R. (1995) *Writing the Future: English and the production of a culture of innovation.* Sheffield: NATE.

Kress, G.R. (1998) 'Visual and verbal modes of representation in electonically mediated communication', in I. Snyder (ed.) *Page to Screen*, London: Routledge.

Lakoff, G. and Johnson, M. (1981) *Metaphors We Live By*, Chicago: University of Chicago Press.

Lanham, Richard (1993) *The Electronic Word: Democracy, technology and the arts*, Chicago: University of Chicago Press.

Laurel, Brenda (1991) *Computers as Theatre: Human–computer interaction*, Reading, MA: Addison-Wesley.

Lowe, Michelle and Graham, Ben (1999) *English Language for Beginners*, London: Writers and Readers.

McEnery, Tony and Wilson, Andrew (1997) *Corpus Linguistics*, Edinburgh: Edinburgh University Press.

McGrath, Melanie (1998) *Hard, Soft and Wet*, London: Flamingo.

Ma, Ringo (1996) 'Computer-mediated conversations as a new dimension of intercultural communication between East Asian and North American college students', in S.C. Herring (ed.) *Computer-Mediated Communication*, Amsterdam: Benjamins.

Malinowski, B. (1923) 'The problem of meaning in primitive languages', in C.K. Ogden and I.A. Richards (eds) *The Meaning of Meaning*, London: Routledge.

Maybin, Janet and Mercer, Neil (1996) *Using English: From conversation to canon*, London: Routledge.

Montgomery, M. (1986) *An Introduction to Language and Society*, London: Routledge.

Moran, Charles and Hawisher, Gail (1998) 'The rhetorics and languages of electronic mail', in I. Snyder (ed.) *Page to Screen*, London: Routledge.

Murray, K.M.E. (1977) *Caught in the Web of Words: J.A.H. Murray and the Oxford English Dictionary*, Oxford: Oxford University Press.

Nash, Walter (1993) *Jargon: Its uses and abuses*, Oxford: Blackwell.

Negroponte, Nicholas (1995) *Being Digital*, London: Coronet.

Nelson, Ted (1987) *Computer Lib/Dream Machines*, Redmond, WA: Tempus Books.

Nelson, Ted (1992) 'Opening hypertext: a memoir', in M. Tuman (ed.) *Literacy On-line: The promise (and peril) of reading and writing with computers*, Pittsburg: University of Pittsburg Press.

The Oxford English Dictionary, 2nd edn on CD-ROM, Oxford: Oxford University Press (online from March 2000); http://www.oed.com

Petrie, Helen (1999) *Writing in Cyberspace: A study of the uses, style and content of e-mail*; http://www.netinvestigations.net/; initial report on http://147.197.156.153/NetResearch/Reports/Email%20Study/InitialReport.htm

Plant, Sadie (1998) *Zeros + Ones: Digital women + the new technoculture*, London: Fourth Estate.

Pope, Rob (1998) *The English Studies Book*, London: Routledge.

Provenzo, Eugene F., Jr (1995) 'The Electronic Panopticon: censorship control and indoctrination in a post typographic culture', in M. Tuman, *Word Perfect*, Chicago: University of Chicago Press.

Raymond, Eric S. (1996) *The New Hackers' Dictionary*, 3rd edn, Cambridge, MA: MIT Press.

Rohrer, Tim (1996) 'Conceptual blending on the Information Highway: how metaphorical inferences work'; http://metaphor.uoregon.edu/iclacnf4.htm

Smith, Marc A. and Kollock, Peter (1996) 'Managing the virtual commons', in S.C. Herring, *Computer-Mediated Communication*, Amsterdam: Benjamins.

Smith, Marc A. and Kollock, Peter (1999) *Communities in Cyberspace*, London: Routledge.

Snyder, Ilana (1998) *Page to Screen: Taking literacy into the electronic era*, London: Routledge.

Spurgeon, Caroline (1952) *Shakespeare's Imagery and What it Tells Us*, Cambridge: Cambridge University Press.

Stanford, Peter (1999) 'Getting the message', *The Sunday Times* 4 July; http://www.sunday-times.co.uk/news/pages/sti/99/07/04/sticulcul02003.html?999

Suler, J. (1999) *The Psychology of Cyberspace*; http://www.rider.edu/users/suler/psycyber/psycyber.html

Tuman, Myron (1992) *Word Perfect: Literacy in the computer age*, Chicago: University of Chicago Press.

Weizenbaum, Joseph (1976) *Computer Power and Human Reason: From judgement to calculation*, W.H. Freeman & Co.

Werry, Christopher (1996) 'Linguistic and interactional features of Internet relay chat', in S.C. Herring (ed.), *Computer-Mediated Communication: Linguistic, social and cross-cultural perspectives*, Amsterdam: Benjamins.

Yates, Simeon (1996) 'English in cyberspace', in S. Goodman and D. Graddol (eds) *Redesigning English*, London: Routledge.

Yates, Simeon (1996) 'Oral and written linguistic aspects of computer conferencing' in S.C. Herring (ed.) *Computer-Mediated Communication*, Amsterdam: Benjamins.

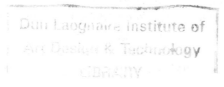